OLD PEWTER

Frontispiece

H. 13"
COMMUNION FLAGON, English. From Midhurst Church, Sussex.

OLD PEWTER
BY MALCOLM BELL

This edition digitally re-mastered and
published by JM Classic Editions © 2008
Original text © Malcolm Bell 1913

ISBN 978-1-905217-47-2

All rights reserved. No part of this book subject
to copyright may be reproduced in any form or
by any means without prior permission in writing
from the publisher.

CONTENTS

CHAPTER		PAGE
	LIST OF ILLUSTRATIONS	vii
	PREFACE	xix
I.	INTRODUCTORY	1
II.	WHAT PEWTER IS	7
III.	HOW PEWTER WAS WROUGHT	24
IV.	PEWTER BEFORE THE FIFTEENTH CENTURY	44
V.	PEWTER IN THE FIFTEENTH CENTURY	63
VI.	PEWTER IN THE SIXTEENTH CENTURY	72
VII.	PEWTER IN THE SEVENTEENTH CENTURY	93
VIII.	THE END OF THE STORY	109
IX.	COLLECTING AND DISPLAYING PEWTER	120
X.	SOME NOTES ON THE ILLUSTRATIONS	147
	A LIST OF USEFUL BOOKS OF REFERENCE	164
	INDEX	165

LIST OF ILLUSTRATIONS

NOTE.—The initials in this list, following the numbers of the plates, denote the ownership of the objects illustrated and are to be read as follows:

A.G.B.—A. G. Bell, Esq.
B.M.—British Museum
B.—Miss Burrell
W.B.—Baillie William Burrell
L.C.—Lewis Clapperton, Esq.
F. & S.—Messrs. Fenton & Sons
G.C.—Glasgow Corporation
B.J.—Mrs. Borough Johnson

M.—Robert Meldrum, Esq.
R.M.—Mrs. Ralston Mitchell
H.M.—H. Murray, Esq.
F.H.N.—F. H. Newbery, Esq.
K.R.—Kennerley Rumford, Esq.
S.K.M.—South Kensington Museum
W.—Mrs. Warren
F.C.Y.—F. C. Yardley, Esq.

PLATE

(S.K.M.) Communion Flagon, English, from Midhurst Church, Sussex   *Frontispiece*

1. (B.M.) Dishes from a hoard of pewter found by Rev. C. H. Engleheart near Roman buildings at Appleshaw, near Andover, Hants, 1897

2. (B.M.) Dishes from a hoard of pewter found by Rev. C. H. Engleheart near Roman buildings at Appleshaw, near Andover, Hants, 1897

3. (B.M.) Vessels and Dish from a hoard of pewter found by Rev. C. H. Engleheart near Roman buildings at Appleshaw, near Andover, Hants, 1897

4. (S.K.M.) The Gloucester Candlestick. XII century

5. (B.) Measure, Pepper-box, Buttons, and Mustard-pot
   1. Measure, German, $4\frac{5}{8}''$ high.
   2. Pepper-box, $5\frac{1}{2}''$ high.
   3. Two Buttons, $2\frac{1}{4}''$ diam.
   4. Mustard-pot, $4''$ high.

6. (W.I.) Pepper-boxes, Sugar-castor, Mustard-pots, and Salt-cellars
   1, 3, 4. Pepper-boxes, $4\frac{1}{2}''$ to $5''$ high.
   2. Sugar-castor, marked with Cupid holding trumpet to mouth with left hand, branch in right, HK, $5\frac{5}{8}''$ high.
   5, 6, 7. Mustard-pots, $3\frac{1}{4}''$ to $5\frac{1}{8}''$ high.
   8, 9, 10, 11, 12. Salt-cellars, $10''$, marked with crowned X.
   Nos. 3, 7, 9 are a set.

OLD PEWTER

PLATE
7. (M.) Bénitier, probably Flemish. No marks
8. (F.C.Y.) Tankards and Tappit Hen
   1. Tankard Flemish. XVII century.
   2. Tappit Hen, Scotch. XVIII century.
   3. Tankard, French. XVIII century.
9. (S.K.M.) Measure, Dish, and Tankard
   1. Measure, English. Early XVIII century.
   2. Dish, English. Middle of XVIII century.
   3. Tankard, English. XVIII century.
10. 1-2. (F. & S.) Bénetiers, Flemish, XVIII century;
    3-4. (F.C.Y.) Bénetiers, Flemish, XVIII century
11. (W.) Toddy Ladles, Soup Ladles, Table-spoons, Fork and Tea-spoon
    1. Toddy Ladles, marked John Yates. VR crowned.
    2. Small fork, no mark. Length 7″.
    3. Soup ladle marked | JO | HN | YA | TES |
    4. Soup ladle, marked | ASK | BER | RY |
       W. crown R.
       BEST METAL
       WARRANTED
       FOR USE
    5. Three table-spoons, marked
        VR crowned.
    6. Tea-spoon, marked A1
       ≶
       Crowned head
       ≶
       PURE
12. (H.M.) Eight Spoons
    1. Laton spoon, 5″ long, found in the Thames at Westminster; an engraved line runs along lower surface of stem. XIV century.
    2. Bronze spoon, 6¼″ long, found in the City of London. XIV century. Probably French.
    3. Laton spoon, 6″ long, French. XIV century.
    4. Laton spoon, 6¾″ long, found in the Thames in London, stem of diamond section. Early XV century.
    5. Laton spoon, 7″ long, found in London. Early XV century. Probably French.
    6. Bronze spoon, 5⅞″ long, found in London. XV century.
    7. Bronze spoon, 6″ long, stem of diamond section, found in London. XV century.
    8. Bronze spoon, 6⅛″ long, found in London. XV century. Mark same as No. 2.

    For marks on these spoons see Plate CIV.

LIST OF ILLUSTRATIONS

PLATE

13. (H.M.) Eight Slip-top Spoons
   1. Pewter slip-top spoon, 6½" long, found at Bermondsey, stem of hexagonal section. XVI century.
   2. Pewter slip-top spoon, 6½" long, found in London. XVI century.
   3. Pewter slip-top spoon, 6¾" long. XVI century.
   4. Pewter slip-top spoon, 6½" long. XVII century.
   5. Pewter slip-top spoon, 6¾" long, found in London. XVI century.
   6. Pewter slip-top spoon, 6" long, found in York Road, Westminster. XVI century.
   7. Pewter slip-top spoon, 6¼" long, found in London. XVI century
   8. Pewter slip-top spoon, 6¼" long, found in London. XVII century.
   For marks on these spoons see Plate CIV.

14. (H.M.) Eight spoons
   1. Pewter spoon, 6½" long, found in London. XVI century.
   2. Pewter spoon, 6¼" long. XVII century.
   3. Laton spoon, 6¾" long, found in London, stem of hexagonal section. XVII century.
   4. Laton spoon, with Apostle top, 6½" long. XVII century.
   5. Pewter spoon, seal headed, hexagonal, 6½" long, found at Bermondsey. XVI century.
   6. Pewter sacramental spoon, with Maidenhead top, 7¼" long, found in London. XVI century.
   7. Pewter spoon, 6½" long, found in London. XVII century.
   8. Pewter spoon, with Apostle top, 6¾" long, found in London. XVI century.
   For marks on these spoons see Plate CIV.

15. (H.M.) Eight Slip-top Spoons
   1. Pewter slip-top spoon, 6" long, found in York Road, Westminster. XVI century. Same marks as Plate XIII, Fig. 6.
   2. Pewter slip-top spoon, 6" long, found in London. XVI century. Same mark as Plate XIII, Fig. 6.
   3. The same as Fig. 2.
   4. Pewter slip-top spoon, 6½" long, found in London. XVI century.
   5. Pewter slip-top spoon, 6¼" long. XVI century.
   6. Pewter slip-top spoon, 6½" long, found in London. XVI century. Same mark as Fig. 2.
   7. Pewter slip-top spoon, 6½" long. XVI century.
   8. Pewter slip-top spoon, 6¾" long, found in Bermondsey. XVI century.
   For marks on these spoons see Plate CV.

16. (H.M.) Nine Slip-top Spoons
   1. Pewter slip-top spoon, 6¾" long, found at Bermondsey. XVI century.
   2. Pewter slip-top spoon, 7¼" long, found in London. XVI century.
   3. Pewter slip-top spoon, 6¾" long, found at Bermondsey. XVI century.
   4. Pewter slip-top spoon, 6½" long, found at Bermondsey. XVI century.
   5. Laton slip-top spoon, 6¼" long, found at Bermondsey, has remains of tin plating. XVII century.
   6. Laton slip-top spoon, 7" long, found at Bermondsey. XVII century.
   7. Laton slip-top spoon, 6 5/16" long, found in London, has remains of tin plating. XVII century.
   8. Pewter slip-top spoon, 6½" long, found in London. XVI century.
   9. Pewter slip-top spoon, 6¾" long, found in London. XVI century.
   For marks on these spoons see Plate CV.

OLD PEWTER

PLATE
17. (H.M.) **Eight Seal-top Spoons**
   1. Laton seal-top spoon, 5¾″ long, found in London. XVII century.
   2. Laton seal-top spoon, 6¼″ long. XVII century.
   3. Laton seal-top spoon, 6¾″ long. XVII century.
   4. Laton seal-top spoon, 6¼″ long, found in London. XVII century.
   5. Laton seal-top spoon, 6³⁄₁₆″ long, found in London. XVII century.
   6. Laton seal-top spoon, 6½″ long, found in London. XVII century.
   7. Laton seal-top spoon, 6⅜″ long, found in London, XVII century.
   8. Laton seal-top spoon, 6⅜″ long, found in London. XVII century.

   For marks on these spoons see Plate CV.

18. (H.M.) **Eight Spoons**
   1. Laton slip-top spoon, 7¾″ long, plated with tin, found in London XVII century.
   2. Pewter slip-top spoon, 7″ long, found at Bermondsey. XVII century.
   3. Laton slip-top spoon, 6¼″ long, found in London. XVII century.
   4. Laton spoon, 7¼″ long, plated with tin. XVII century.
   5. Laton spoon, 5⅝″ long, with remains of tin plating. XVII century.
   6. Laton spoon, 7¼″ long, plated with tin. Handle "Pied de Biche." Mark same as Fig. 5.
   7. Laton spoon, 7⅜″ long, with remains of tin plating. Handle "Pied de Biche." XVII century.
   8. Laton rat-tailed spoon, 7¼″ long, found in York Road, Westminster. Handle "Pied de Biche." XVII century.

   For marks on these spoons see Plate CVI.

19. (H.M.) **Nine Rat-tailed Spoons**
   1. Laton rat-tailed spoon, 8″ long, plated with tin. Handle "Pied de Biche." XVII century.
   2. Pewter rat-tailed spoon, 7¼″ long, found in Newgate Street. Handle "Pied de Biche." XVII century.
   3. Laton rat-tailed spoon, 7″ long, found in York Road, Westminster, plated with tin. XVII century.
   4. Pewter rat-tailed spoon, 7¾″ long, found in Bermondsey. XVII century.
   5. Pewter rat-tailed spoon, 7¾″ long, found in Bermondsey. XVII century.
   6. Pewter rat-tailed spoon, 7″ long. XVII century.
   7. Laton spoon, 5⅝″ long, plated with pewter, found in London. Late XVII century.
   8. Bronze rat-tailed spoon, 5¾″ long. XVII century.
   9. Rat-tailed pewter chocolate spoon, 4″ long, found in the Wandle at Wandsworth. XVII century.

   For marks on these spoons see Plate CVI.

20. (H.M.) **Eight Spoons and Ladles**
   1. Pewter spoon, 8½″ long, found in London. Late XVIII century.
   2. Laton dog-nose gravy spoon, 10¾″ long, plated with tin. XVII century.
   3. Pewter spoon, 7¾″ long, found in Bermondsey. Late XVIII century.
   4. Laton slip-top ladle, 8¾″ long, the handle of hexagonal section. XVII century.

LIST OF ILLUSTRATIONS

PLATE

   5. Laton slip-top ladle, 8″ long, found in the City of London, has remains of tin plating. XVII century.
   6. Laton slip-top ladle, 7¼″ long, found in Suffolk. XVII century.
   7. Laton slip-top handle, 6½″ long, found in London. XVII century.
   8. Laton spoon, seal-headed, 6½″ long, has remains of tin plating, found at Norwich. XVII century.

   For marks on these spoons see Plate CVI.

21. (S.K.M.) Pyx, Communion Flagon, Chalice, and Paten
   1. Hexagonal Pyx, English. XIV century.
   2. Communion Flagon, English. From Midhurst Church, Sussex, 1677.
   3. Chalice and Paten. From Kriswick.

22. (S.K.M.) Communion Flagon, Alms Dish, and Patens
   1. Communion Flagon, English. XVII century.
   2. Alms Dish, Scotch. XVIII century. Marked AS. IK.
   3. Patens from a Church in Yorkshire. English. XV century.

23. (B.) Church Flagon, Scotch, early XVIII century type

24. (F.C.V.) Alms Dish, Chalice, and Laver
   1. Alms Dish, English. XVIII century.
   2. Chalice, English. XVIII century.
   3. Laver, Scotch. Late XVIII century.

25. (W.) Communion Jug and Two Chalices
   1. Chalice, Italian.
   2. Earthenware Communion Jug, mounted in pewter.
   3. Chalice, Scotch.

26. (K.R.) Two Chalices and Church Flagon, English

27. (F. & S.) Three Chalices, English, XVIII century

28. (L.C.) Loving Cup, Communion Cup, and Porringer
   1. Loving Cup, English.
   2. Communion Cup, Scotch.
   3. Porringer, French. Probably XVII century.

29. (G.C.) Communion Cup, Spice-box, and Candlestick
   1. Communion Cup. 1804.
   2. Spice-box, French. XVIII century.
   3. Candlestick, French. XVIII century.

30. Pocket Communion Service, Sacramental Cruets, and Measure
   1. (L.C.) Pocket Communion Service in wooden case, bought in Iceland. Probably Danish or Scotch.
   2. (F. & S.) Sacramental Cruet, Aqua. French or Flemish.
   3. (F. & S.) Measure, *temp.* Charles II. Found in Parliament Street, Westminster.
   4. (F. & S.) Sacramental Cruet, Vinum. French or Flemish.

OLD PEWTER

PLATE
31. (W.) Sacramental Cruet and Five Measures
    1. Cruet, Vinum.
    2. Gill Measure, modern.
    3. Half Mutchkin Measure.
    4. Old Half-glass Measure.
    5. Half-gill Measure.
    6. Gill Measure.

32. (B.) Altar Candlesticks and German Guild Cup, XVII century
    1, 3. Two Altar Candlesticks.
    2. German Guild Cup.

33. (F. & S.) Two Altar Candlesticks, Flemish, XVII century

34. (R.M.) Candelabrum, Flemish, XVIII century

35. (W.B.) Alms Dish, German, early XVIII century

36. (W.) Candlesticks
    1. A pair of Pillar Candlesticks, Scotch. XVIII century.
    2. Flat Candlestick, Scotch. XIX century.
    3. A pair of Pillar Candlesticks, Dutch. XVIII century.

37. (F. & S.) Oil lamps, Taper Holder, and Candlestick
    1, 4, 5. Oil Lamps, German. XVIII century.
    2. Taper Holder, Flemish.
    3. Pillar Candlestick, French.

38. Lamp Time-keepers
    1. (A.G.B.) Lamp Time-keeper. XVII century.
    2. (F.C.V.) Lamp Time-keeper. XVII century.
    3, 4, 5. (B.) Lamp Time-keepers. XVII century.

39. (F.C.V.) Three Pillar Candlesticks

40. (R.M.) Pillar Candlesticks, Tray, and Inkstand
    1, 4. A pair of Pillar Candlesticks. XVIII century.
    2. Tray. XVIII century.
    3. Inkstand.

41. (W.) Drinking Cups
    1. Cup, Scotch. XVIII century.
    2. Loving Cup. XVIII century.
    3. A pair of Wine Cups. XVIII century.

42. (M.) Three German Guild Cups
    1. Cup, on lid 1721, three shields, right and left a tankard, above I.W.L. below 1713, centre one a church with spire.
    2. Flagon, on front IMS 1706, Nuremberg rose on bottom inside, on the handle a shield, IMK, a wall and two turrets.
    3. Cup, inscribed Johannes George Reichel Johannes Battzer Rellurg, Anno 1693, Christope Stutz.

LIST OF ILLUSTRATIONS

PLATE
43. (R.M.) Flagons and Beaker
    1. Flagon, German. XVIII century.
    2. Beaker, Scotch. XVIII century.
    3. Flagon, German. XVIII century.

44. (F. & S.) Tankard, Measures, and Beaker
    1. Tankard, Scotch. XVIII century.
    2, 3. Measures, English. Early XVIII century.
    4. Beaker, engraved. Early XVIII century. Mark, a crowned rose.

45. (R.M.) Dishes and Tankard
    1. Dish, English. XVII century.
    2. Tankard, German. XVIII century.
    3. Deep Dish, Scotch. XVI century.

46. (W.B.) Four Tankards, German, XVII century
47. (W.B.) Three Tankards, German, XVII and XVIII centuries
48. (S.K.M.) Tankards and Jug
    1. Peg Tankard, Danish. With engraved decoration.
    2. Jug, English. XVIII century.
    3. Tankard, Swedish. 1844.

49. (S.K.M.) Ewer, Cruet Stand, and Guild Tankard
    1. Ewer and Cover, German.
    2. Cruet Stand, German. Middle of XVIII century.
    3. Guild Tankard, German. Dated 1645.

50. (F. & S.) Cream-jugs, Salt-cellar, Measure, and Egg Cup
    1, 5. Two Cream-jugs.
    2. Salt-cellar.
    3. Measure.
    4. Egg Cup. All English. XVIII century.

51. (W.B.) A pair of Covered Tankards, German, XVIII century
52. (W.B.) Three German Guild Tankards
53. (W.B.) Three German Guild Tankards, XVII to XVIII century
54. (S.K.M.) Measure or Tankard, German, late XVII century
55. (G.C.) Four Measures, Scotch, XVIII century
56. (G.C.) Five Measures
57. (S.K.M.) Wine Taster and Measures
    1. Wine-Taster, English. XVII century. Dug up in Tottenham Court Road.
    2, 3. Wine Measures, German. XVIII century.

OLD PEWTER

PLATE

58. (F.C.Y.) Bowl, Water-jug, Rice Boiler, Plate, and Measure
    1. Two-handled Bowl.
    2. Water-jug, English. XVIII century.
    3. Rice Boiler, French. XVIII century.
    4. Plate, English. XVIII century. One of a set of six.
    5. Measure, English. XVIII century.

59. (F. & S.) Set of eight French Measures, XVIII century

60. (R.M.) Tappit Hen, XVIII century

61. (W.) Three Tappit Hens

62. (F.C.Y.) Jug, English, XVII century

63. (W.B.) Flagons
    1. Flagon, probably Scotch. XVIII century.
    2. Imitation Chinese Flagon, Dutch. XVII century.
    3. Flagon, German. XVII century.

64. (G.C.) Jugs and Flagon
    1. Covered Jug. Archangel mark.
    2. Flagon.
    3. Cream-jug.

65. (F.C.Y.) Bowls, Dish, and Plate
    1 and 4. A pair of Two-handled bowls.
    2. Dish, English. Dated 1689.
    3. Plate, English. XVIII century. One of six.

66. (W.) Jugs
    1. Jug, French. XVIII century.
    2. Jug, English. XVIII century.
    3. Beer-jug, English. XVIII century.

67. (F.C.Y.) Jugs and Coffee-pot
    1. Jug, Dutch. Marked crossed rose.
    2. Coffee-pot, Dutch. No marks.
    3. Jug, Dutch. Mark, a rose within a circle of illegible lettering.

68. (B.J.) Jug, George IV.

69. (F.C.Y.) Bowls
    1. Barber's Bowl, English. XVIII century.
    2. Two-handled Bowl, Dutch. XVIII century.

70. (F.C.Y.) Three Porringers

71. (W.) Bowls and Casket
    1. Two-handled Bowl, Scotch.
    2. Casket, French. XVI century.
    3. Two-handled Bowl.

LIST OF ILLUSTRATIONS

PLATE

72. (F.C.V.) Mustard-pot, Jug, and Measure
    1. Mustard-pot, English. XVII century.
    2. Hot-water Jug, Dutch. Early XVIII century.
    3. Measure, English. Early XVIII century.

73. (F.C.V.) Salver, Jugs, Dish, and Plate
    1. Wavy-edged Salver, with feet, Dutch. Late XVIII century.
    2. Student's Beer-jug, German. XVII century.
    3. Dish, English. XVIII century.
    4. Water-jug, English. Late XVIII century.
    5. Wavy-edged Plate, English. Late XVIII century. One of a set of six.

74. (F.C.V.) Tankards, Dish, Mug, Measure, and Tobacco-box
    1. Tankard, English. Early XVIII century.
    2. Dish, Scotch, stamped with initials A. D. V. and A. W. XVI century.
    3. Mug with handle, English. Early XVIII century.
    4. Measure, English. XVII century.
    5. Tankard, English. XVIII century.
    6. Tobacco-box, English. XVIII century.

75. (G.C.) Soup Tureen, Russian. Archangel mark

76. (F.C.V.) Vegetable Dish, Tray, and Jugs
    1. Vegetable Dish, English. Late XVIII century.
    2. Tray or Salver, Dutch.
    3. Milk-jug, English. Late XVIII century.
    4. Water-jug, English. XVIII century.

77. (R.M.) Ewer and Basin

78. (F.C.V.) Bowl and Jug
    1. Bowl, Flemish. XVII century.
    2. Jug, Dutch. Early XVIII century.

79. (B.J.) Mustard-pots, Salt-cellar, Pepper-box, and Measure
    1 and 3. Mustard-pots. XVIII century.
    2. Salt-cellar. XVIII century.
    4. Pepper-box. XVIII century.
    5. Measure. XVIII century.

80. (F. & S.) 1–6. Mustard-pots, XVII and XVIII centuries

81. (F. & S.) 1–6. Pepper-pots, XVII and XVIII centuries

82. (L.C.) Cream-jug, Salt-cellars, Measure, and Spoons
    1. Cream-jug, Scotch.
    3, 5, 7. Three Salt-cellars, English.
    9. Quarter-gill Measure. Glasgow mark.
    2, 4, 6, 8, 10. Five Spoons, Dutch.

OLD PEWTER

PLATE
83. (R.M.) Measure, Salt-cellar, Sugar-castor, Cruet, and Inkstand
   1. Measure.
   2. Salt-cellar.
   3. Sugar-castor.
   4. Vinegar Cruet.
   5. Inkstand.

84. (F.C.Y.) Five Salt-cellars

85. (F.H.N.) Sugar-sifters, Cruets, and Spirit Lamp
   1, 2. Sugar-sifters. XVIII century.
   3, 4, 5. Set of Cruets, Scotch. XVIII century.
   6. Spirit Lamp.

86. (W.) Cream-jugs, Herb Cannisters, and Box
   1. Cream-jug, Scotch.
   2. Herb Cannister, Dutch. XVII century.
   3. Box.
   4. Herb Cannister, Dutch. Marked 1766
   5. Cream-jug.

87. (F. & S.) Urns
   1. Dutch Urn.
   2. French Urn. XVIII century.
   3. Dutch Urn.

88. (B.J.) Tea-pot, Cream-jug, and Coffee-pot
   1. Tea-pot. Early XIX century.
   2. Cream-jug. Early XIX century.
   3. Coffee-pot. XVIII century

89. (B.) Tea-pots and Coffee-pot
   1. Tea-pot, Dutch. XVIII century.
   2. Coffee-pot, French. XVIII century.
   3. Tea-pot, Flemish. XVIII century.

90. (S.K.M.) Coffee-pot, Sugar-box, and Mustard-pot
   1. Coffee-pot, Louis XIV style, German. First half XVIII century.
   2. Sugar-box and Cover, Dutch. Dated 1751.
   3. Mustard-pot.

91 (W.) Egg Cups
   1, 2, 3. Egg Cups. No marks.
   4, 5, 6, 7, 8, 9. Set of Six Egg Cups, Scotch. No marks.

92. (F.C.Y.) Milk-jug, Sugar-basin, and Tea-pot
   1. Milk-jug, English. Early XIX century.
   2. Sugar-basin, English. Early XIX century.
   3. Tea-pot, English. Early XIX century.

93. (K.R.) Tea-pot and Tankard
   1. Tea-pot. Early XIX century.
   2. Tankard, English. XVIII century.

LIST OF ILLUSTRATIONS

PLATE
94. (B.J.) Tea-pots and Tobacco-box
    1. Tea-pot. Early XIX century.
    2. Tea-pot. XVIII century.
    3. Tobacco-box. XVIII century.

95. (K.R.) Coffee-pot, Inkstand, and Tobacco-box
    1. Coffee-pot, Flemish. XVIII century.
    2. Inkstand, French. XVIII century.
    3. Tobacco-box, French. XVIII century.

96. (W.) Snuff-boxes and Shoe-buckles
    1, 3, 5. Three Snuff-boxes.
    2, 4. A Pair of Shoe-buckles, the forks of hand-cut steel.

97. (F.C.V.) Pepper-pots, Mustard-pot, Snuff-box, and Egg Cup.
    1, 2. Two Pepper-pots.
    3. Mustard-pot, English. Early XVIII century.
    4. Snuff-box, English. Middle XVIII century.
    5. Egg Cup, with Bead Pattern, English. XVIII century.

98. (W.) Ink-pot, Inkstand, and Tobacco-box
    1. Ink-pot, Scotch.
    2. Inkstand, Italian.
    3. Tobacco-box.

99. (F.H.N.) Flagons and Inkstand
    1. Flagon. XVII century.
    2. Inkstand. Late XVIII century.
    3. Flagon. XVII century.

100. (W.) Oriental Dagger. Handle of Pewter and Bone. Top and bottom of sheath bound with pewter

101. (W.B.) Food Bottles and Salt-box
    1, 3. Food Bottles.
    2. Salt-box.

102. (A.G.B.) Shaving-pot, Sugar-sprinklers, Jug, and Sugar-basin
    1. Shaving-pot, English.
    2, 4. A pair of Sugar-sprinklers, Belgian.
    3. Cider-jug, Norman.
    5. Sugar-basin, Belgian.

103. (B.J.) Mugs, Flagon, and Tankard
    1. Mug, William IV.
    2. Flagon. XVIII century.
    3. Tankard. Late XVIII century.
    4. Mug. Early XIX century.

104. (H.M.) Marks on Spoons
105. (H.M.) Marks on Spoons
106. (H.M.) Marks on Spoons

PREFACE

IN compiling the present volume I have not attempted to disguise from myself the fact that however keen my own interest in the subject may be, it is destined to appeal to the public far more by its numerous and carefully chosen illustrations than by anything I may have to say. I make no pretence of laying before the reader any entirely novel discoveries concerning pewter. To Mr. Starkie Gardner's paper in the "Journal of the Society of Arts," to Mr. Welch's "History of the Pewterers' Company," to Mr. Massé's "Pewter Plate," especially to the extremely useful Bibliography contained in it, and to Mr. Ingleby Wood's "Scottish Pewter-ware and Pewterers," I freely and gratefully acknowledge my indebtedness for the main portion of the facts herein set forth; and I

cannot too strongly recommend those whom the present volume may haply attract for the first time to a care for pewter and its history to seek fuller instruction in their pages. I have merely endeavoured to gather here such information as may enable the inexperienced to study the pictures with eyes not altogether unopened to their meaning, in the hope that a first taste of this particular well of knowledge, however ill-served, may tempt them to fuller and deeper draughts elsewhere; and if I succeed in this much I shall not deem myself to have altogether failed.

In conclusion there only remains to me the pleasant task of thanking most heartily on my own behalf, as well, I trust, as on behalf of any readers I may have, those ladies and gentlemen who have so generously allowed their treasures to be photographed and reproduced, namely Mrs. Warren, Mrs. Ralston Mitchell, Mrs. Borough Johnson, Miss Burrell, Mr. Arthur G. Bell, Mr. William Burrell, Mr. Lewis Clapperton, Messrs. Fenton and Sons, Mr. Robert Meldrum, Mr. H. Murray, Mr.

PREFACE

F. H. Newbery, Mr. Kennerley Rumford, Mr. Frank C. Yardley, and the authorities of the British Museum, the Victoria and Albert Museum, and the Glasgow Corporation Museum. I have also to express my grateful thanks to Mr. Yardley for cordial and invaluable assistance in the preparation of this work, particularly in the selection and dating of objects for reproduction, and to Mr. Hugh P. Bell for the information concerning the chemical analysis of pewter.

MALCOLM BELL.

OLD PEWTER

THE FIRST CHAPTER

INTRODUCTORY

OOKED at rightly the rapid growth of the quite modern taste for collecting the many various objects formerly fashioned of pewter must be regarded as among the healthiest symptoms of the later art development in Europe. It is, in the first place, a genuine unaffected taste, not a mere fashionable craze; nor, if one may venture to formulate a prophecy concerning matters so independent of any rational foundation as the freaks of popular fancy are apt to be, is it ever likely to become so. The key-note of the fascination of pewter at its best is its simplicity. It appeals to the eye by delicate and subtle balances of line and proportion and has nothing in it of the obvious and sensational. It does not, like gold and silver plate, hint in any way at large intrinsic

values, nor has it their aggressive sparkle and glitter clamouring decoratively for attention. Neither does it lend itself sympathetically to that elaborate manipulation by dexterous craft which attracts by its sheer elaboration and ingenuity the unreasoned approbation of the vulgar; its high lights are too subdued, its shadows too mellowed, to repay by brilliancy of effect for excessive labour, while the softness of the material is such that where this has been bestowed mistakenly the necessarily constant polishing soon wears away the sharpness. It depends upon its construction, not on its added ornamentation; and, as too much modern architecture makes evident, a refined sense of proportion, an appreciation of the importance of restful spaces, are, for some reason, yearly becoming more rare among us, though for them no superabundance of lavish decoration, however good in itself, can compensate. It has not, again, the fascinating fragility of china, glass, and earthenware, which makes the joy of possessing them, to quote Mr. Gilbert, "a pleasure that's almost pain." Lastly, in the history of pewter there are no great names or conspicuous schools for the speculative dealer to boom into fictitious

PLATE I

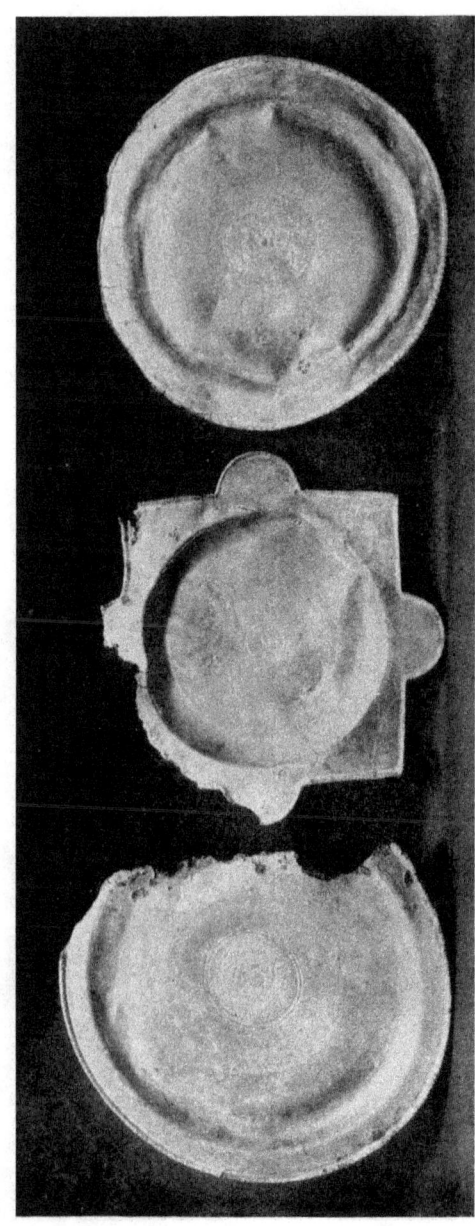

1 D. 15¾"   2 D. 14½"   3 D. 14¾"

DISHES from a hoard of pewter found by Rev. C. H. Engleheart near Roman buildings at Appleshaw, near Andover, Hants, 1897.

PLATE II

1 D. 17″   2 D. 19″

DISHES, from a hoard of pewter found by Rev. C. H. Engleheart near Roman buildings at Appleshaw, near Andover, Hants, 1897.

INTRODUCTORY

and precarious popularity which serves only in the end to unjustifiably inflate prices. The works of Briot and Enderlein and some few other makers may perhaps be brought forward in exception to this statement, but for reasons more fully entered into later these will be accorded but brief notice in these pages. An understanding of the finest work done in pewter implies an approbation of good work honestly applied, of sound design based on actual needs, of unassuming worth, not pretentious value; and these are not qualities commonly held in estimation by the bearers of the longest purses in the auction-rooms.

Fifty years ago, or even less, had any one been at the pains of giving the matter a thought, the utter disappearance of all old domestic pewter, except from a few houses where the former plenishings were preserved more out of habit or curiosity than from any real knowledge of their beauty, might have seemed to be within measurable distance, while far more recently fine church pewter has been melted down or thoughtlessly allowed to vanish in favour of modern white metal or plated abominations. Who first revived an interest in these fast diminishing relics of the past may already be past discovery, but of late the number of his followers has increased annually, and pewter is now firmly established as one of the subjects fully deserving a literature to itself.

Much has already been elicited by patient research and not a little written, and the time is drawing near, if indeed it has not arrived, when any new volume on the matter may be asked to show justification for its existence.

In the present instance the number of reproductions of carefully selected and well-authenticated typical examples must be placed in the first line of defence. To the beginner in the study of any branch of art production the opportunity of examining specimens of generally recognised merit is all-essential, yet in few is this so difficult of attainment as in the case of pewter. Indeed, unless the novice is fortunate enough to be acquainted with the owner of a good collection, it may be said to be practically impossible. In our museums attention has been almost exclusively confined to articles showing more or less laborious ornamentation, which are beside our purpose, while the plainer articles of every-day use have been well-nigh ignored. It is hoped that our illustrations will to some extent remedy this defect. That

INTRODUCTORY

no object shall be brought under the collector's notice to which a fairly close parallel for comparison cannot be found in these pages is too much to expect, but every effort has been made to render the variety of forms and periods as catholic and extensive as possible. With regard to the letterpress, an attempt, however inadequate, has been made to compress into a volume of convenient size all the more important of the facts that are known, and these have been at times supplemented by earnestly weighed, though maybe erroneous, conjectures.

We begin, in our second chapter, with a consideration of what pewter is, indicating the chief divergences in the alloys, and pointing out various methods of estimating the nature of the one present in any given object, either roughly for general use, or more precisely by chemical analysis for the scientifically minded inquirer. In the next chapter the different ways in which the metal was wrought into shape, and the conditions under which this was usually done, are briefly described without dwelling with unnecessary prolixity on technical details. In the five succeeding chapters some of the most striking features in the history of pewter and pewterers, as far as known, are sketched, while the ninth chapter is devoted to such suggestions as it is practicable to offer—far too few and insufficient, unfortunately—which may serve to smooth to some extent the path of the beginner in collecting and effectively displaying his pewter. The tenth and final chapter is devoted to a brief indication of the leading features in the illustrations. If this work, despite its too probable errors and omissions, should succeed in arousing in but a few hitherto indifferent minds an intelligent interest in the rare æsthetic qualities of old domestic or ecclesiastical pewter-ware, the author will be amply rewarded.

PLATE III

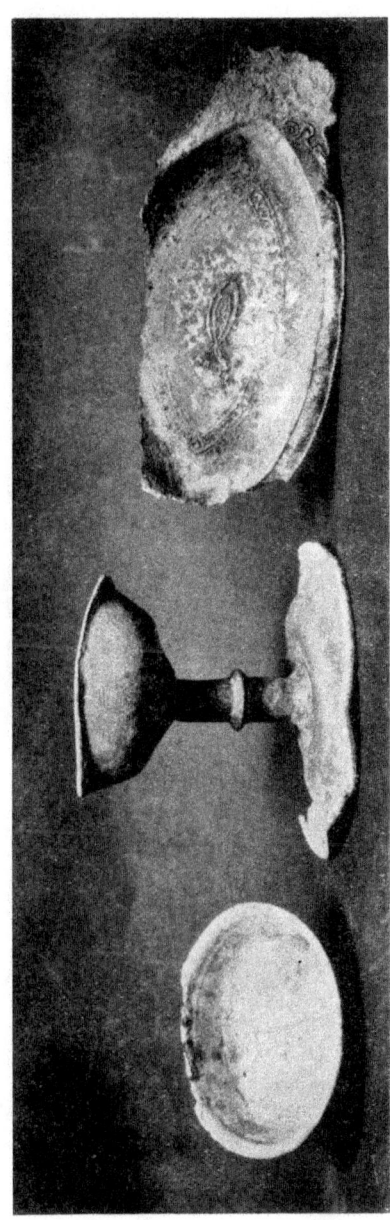

1 D. 4"   2 D. 5"   3 D. 7½"

VESSELS AND DISH from a hoard of pewter found by Rev. C. H. Engleheart near Roman buildings at Appleshaw, near Andover, Hants, 1897.

PLATE IV

H. 22¼"
THE GLOUCESTER CANDLESTICK
XII century.

THE SECOND CHAPTER
WHAT PEWTER IS

EWTER—the word which, with the pleasing independence of rigid orthographic rules that characterises all mediæval English documents, whether lay, legal, or clerical, appears under the widely varying but always recognisable guises of pewtre, peautre, pewtir, peutre, peuther, and even pewder and pewdre—is confidently asserted by Doctor Johnson to owe its derivation to the Dutch peauter. Professor Skeat, on the other hand, the weight of whose opinion cannot well be over-estimated, suggests in his Etymological Dictionary as, at any rate, a strong probability, that the fact is the exact contrary, and that the Dutch word, together with the old French peutre, peautre or piautre, the Italian peltro and the Spanish peltre, are all borrowed from the English word, which is itself an adaptation of spelter; nor is the question without a certain importance, since in the case of a purely artificial compound of this description a not unreasonable presumption

is that the place of its origin, at all events as far as Western civilisation is concerned, coincides with the land which first gave it a name.

The word, however, as applied to the material, can only be regarded as generic, not specific. It signifies always an alloy of two or more metals in which tin forms the preponderating element, but the added components are so varied in their nature and so diverse in their proportions, while the resulting compounds are so different in qualities and appearance, that Mr. Starkie Gardner, attempting in an admirable paper read before the Society of Arts on May 8, 1894, to decide to what exactly the name pewter should be applied, could only say, "the proportions are so variable that it is scarcely possible to exclude any in which tin forms the bulk, where the result is a darkish silvery, soft metal, fusible at a low temperature, inexpensive, and eminently adapted to a variety of household and artistic purposes"; a definition which cannot be said to err on the side of narrowness. Yet any endeavour to further restrict it leads straightway to contradiction. A passage in Mr. Massé's instruc-

DESCRIPTIONS OF OBJECTS ON PLATE V.

1. Measure, German, $4\frac{7}{8}''$ high.
2. Pepper box, $5\frac{1}{2}''$ high.
3. Two buttons, $2\frac{1}{4}''$ diam.
4. Mustard pot, $4''$ high.

DESCRIPTIONS OF OBJECTS ON PLATE VI.

1, 3, 4. Pepper boxes, $4\frac{1}{2}''$ to $5''$ high.
2. Sugar castor, marked with Cupid holding trumpet to mouth with left hand, branch in right, HK, $5\frac{5}{8}''$ high.
5, 6, 7. Mustard pots, $3\frac{1}{2}''$ to $5\frac{1}{8}''$ high.
8, 9, 10, 11, 12. Salt cellars, $10''$, marked with crowned X.
Nos. 3, 7, 9 are a set.

PLATE V

1   2   4
3

PLATE VI

     1   2   3   4
     5   6   7
8   9   10   11   12

For Descriptions, see back of plates.

WHAT PEWTER IS

tive volume on Pewter Plate (p. 20) implies that from his point of view "pewter of good quality . . . should contain no lead," while according to Mr. Starkie Gardner, strictly speaking, lead alone should be added, and his recipe has at least the support of antiquity, for of this nature was all the old Roman pewter analysed by Mr. Gowland and others. In an important appendix to a paper, printed in *Archæologia* in 1898, describing the remains of a Roman villa and a number of contemporary pewter vessels unearthed at Appleshaw, to which further reference will be made later on, he discussed and tabulated all the analyses of Roman pewter that were available. The results show on the surface an extraordinary divergency, the fifteen samples tested ranging with considerable regularity from a mixture of 99.18 of tin with .14 of lead, or practically pure tin, and a probably accidental trace of iron, down to a blend of 45.74 of tin and 53.34 of lead with traces of iron and copper, but Mr. Gowland in his luminous comment makes it clear "that this irregularity is more apparent than real." " If we now examine the analyses in the table," he argues, "we will find that the greater number of the specimens may be placed in one or other of the two following groups, A and B, each characterised by a special percentage of tin—Group A having an average composition of: tin 71.5, lead 27.8; Group B with an average composition of: tin 78.2, lead 21.7"; and he further points out that, as far as the small number of analyses permitted us to judge, "the first was most generally employed by the Romans during their occupation of Britain," a deduction which remarkably agrees with the analysis of some dating from the fourth century found at Aquæ Neriæ, which, according to Bapst, contains tin and lead in the proportions of about 7 to 3. In conclusion Mr. Gowland remarks: "It is worthy of note that the most tenacious alloy of tin and lead closely approaches these Roman pewters in composition, a fact which bears important testimony to the knowledge of the properties of metals possessed by the Romans. In the preparation of these two pewters the Romans seem to have followed the practice, which still survives in some foundries, of taking 1 pound (libra) of the chief metal and allotting the quantity of the other metal to be mixed with it in the sub-divisions of a pound (unciæ).

PLATE VII

B. 7"

BÉNITIER, Probably Flemish.
No marks.

PLATE VIII

1 H. 8¾"
TANKARD, Flemish.
XVII century.

2 H. 12½"
TAPPIT HEN, Scotch.
XVIII century.

3 H. 7½"
TANKARD, French.
XVIII century.

WHAT PEWTER IS

Thus the pewter of Group A was evidently made by melting together 1 libra of tin with $4\frac{1}{2}$ unciæ of lead, which, with due allowance for the oxidation of part of the tin, would yield an alloy of that composition. Pewter B was similarly the result of melting 1 libra of tin with 3 unciæ of lead"; and he finally calls attention to the fact that of two cakes of unwrought metal of Roman make found in the Thames at Battersea, one agrees in composition with Group A, the other with Group B, which circumstance can only be regarded as convincing evidence that his reasoning is sound.

In later days, however, other metals were very generally employed in place of, or in addition to, the lead, as is shown by other analyses also carried out by Mr. Gowland. Thus the English "fine pewter" contains 112 parts of tin to 26 of copper and no lead at all; "better pewter" of the first quality 84 of tin, 7 of antimony, and 4 of copper; of third quality 56 of tin, 8 of lead, 6 of copper, and 2 of zinc; "plate pewter" of the second quality contains only tin and antimony in the proportion of 112 to 6 or 7; while that of the third quality consisted of 90 parts of tin, 7 of antimony, 2 of copper, and 2 of bismuth. The use of brass or copper was actually enforced, for certain purposes, by the ordinances drawn up for the guidance of pewterers in 1348, wherein the "fine pewter" referred to above is described as tin mixed with copper (or brass) "as much as of its own nature it will take," *i.e.*, about 1 part to 4, and at the same time the articles to be made of this alloy, chiefly those that were made square or ribbed, are definitely prescribed, while, writing more than two hundred years later, Harrison, in a "Description of England in Shakespeare's Youth," when eulogising English pewterers and pewter, says: "I have also been informed that it consisteth of a composition which hath 30 lbs. of kettle-brass to 1000 lbs. of tin, whereunto they add 3 or 4 lbs. of tin-gloss (in modern parlance, bismuth); but as too much of this doth make the stuff brickle, so the more the brass be the better is the pewter, and more profitable unto him that doth buy and purchase the same."

The proportion of lead legalised by the same ordinances for the blending of what we may with Mr. Gardner's support be allowed perhaps to entitle true pewter, which was to be used

WHAT PEWTER IS

for making "pots rounded, cruets rounded, candlesticks and other rounded vessels," was 22 pounds according to one account, 26 according to another, for each hundredweight of tin, though there would seem to have been some laxity in carrying out this regulation, since only two years later, in 1350, certain proceedings at the Guildhall indicate that the then customary blend was only 16 pounds of lead to 112 of tin. Small variations, in fact, within reasonable limits were evidently not considered of great importance, and every centre of the industry was a law unto itself. The Montpelier pewterers, for example, in 1437 used a mixture of 96 parts of tin to 4 of lead for dishes and porringers, 90 of tin and 10 of lead for ewers and salts, while the Limoges pewterers mixed 100 parts of tin with only 4 of lead; the Nuremberg pewterers were required in 1576 to use 10 pounds of tin to every 1 of lead; finally, in France, during the eighteenth century 100 parts of tin were mixed either with 5 parts of copper, or with 3 of copper and 1 of bismuth, or with 15 parts of lead, though at the present day a percentage of 16.5 of lead with a narrow margin for error is alone authorised as safe for the storage of wine.

OLD PEWTER

The object of these regulations in every case was, in the first place to ensure sufficient wearing power in the article, and in the second, to protect the customer from adulteration and consequent deterioration of the alloy by an excessive amount of lead, the cheaper component, and so long as the quantity of this used was kept within limits, the addition of other materials would seem to have been left to a considerable extent to the fancy of the individual worker, who varied his composition according to the purpose to which it was to be applied, a liberty which was probably further secured to him in early days by the imperfection of chemical science, and its inability to segregate minute percentages from samples of small weight.

Even in these days of prodigiously improved methods the true ingredients of any given example cannot be regarded as ascertained with any very near approach to accuracy by an analysis of single scrapings or other comparatively infinitesimally small proportions of the whole bulk. In the course of the discussion which followed the reading of the paper by Mr. Starkie Gardner, quoted above, Mr. Gowland stated that in analysing two

PLATE IX

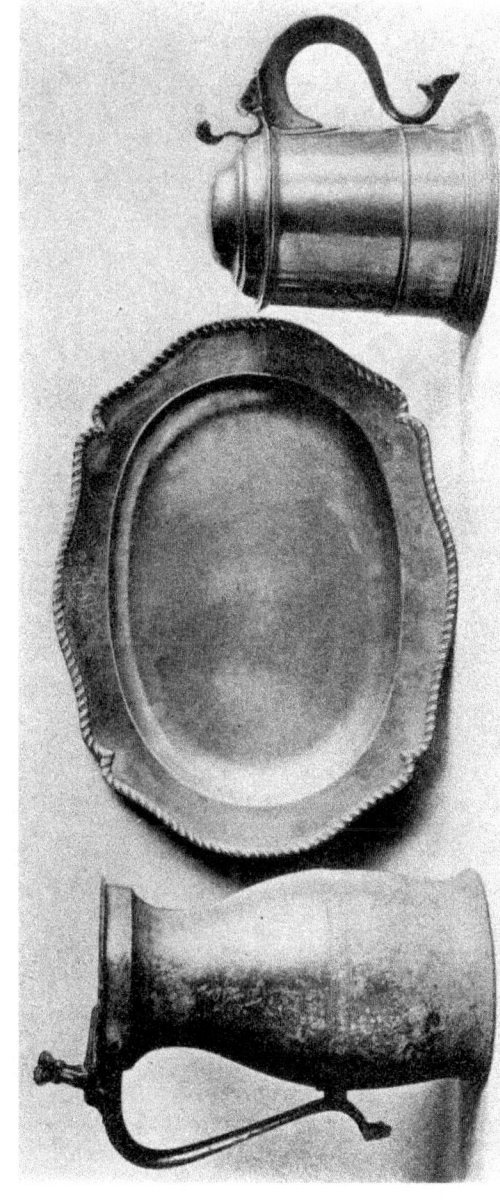

1 H. 15"
MEASURE. English. Early XVIII century. Mark on lid "John Home" Snow Hill, London. On lip T M 1716.

2 L. 17 1/8" W. 13 1/8"
DISH. The rim engraved with a shield of arms surrounded by rococo scroll-work and foliage. English. Middle of XVIII century.

3 H. 8 3/4"
TANKARD. Engraved with IAM beneath an anchor. Mark Pitt & Dadley with a bird. English. XVIII century.

PLATE X

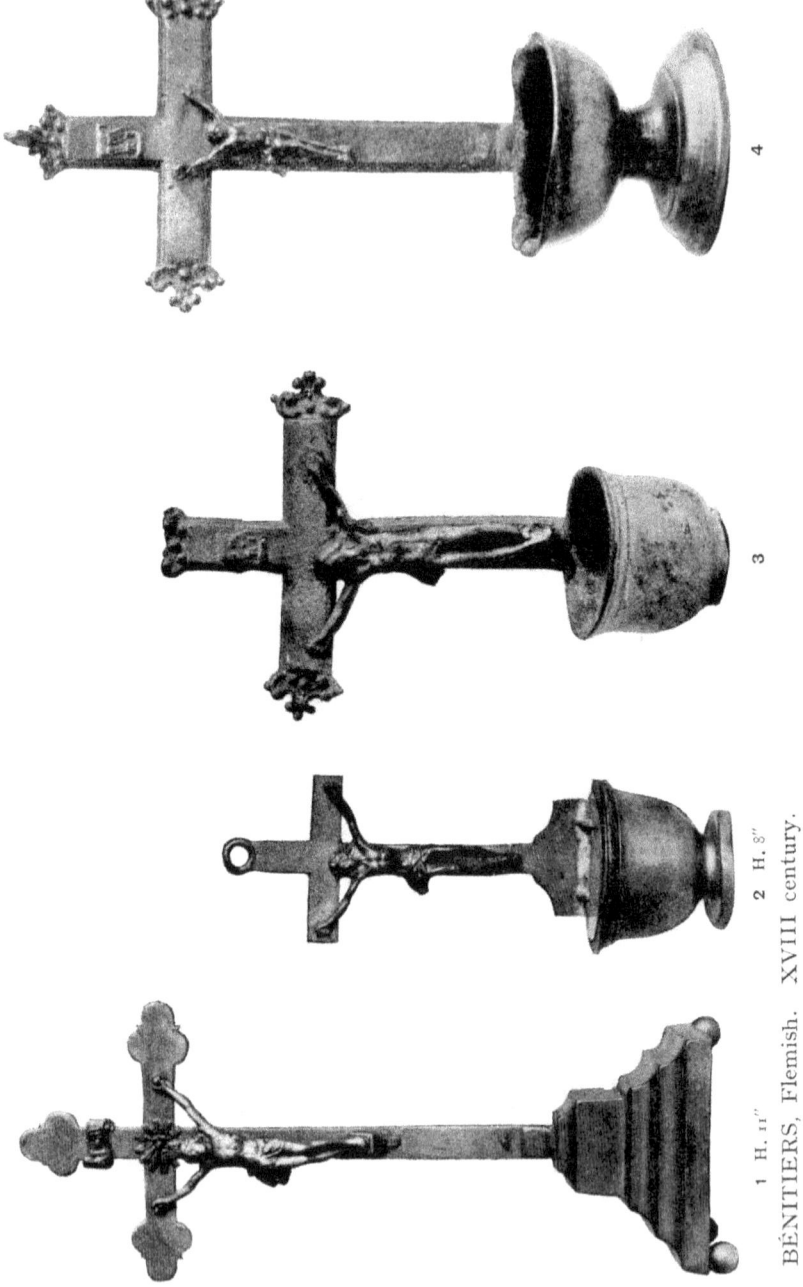

1 H. 11″   2 H. 8″
BÉNITIERS, Flemish. XVIII century.

WHAT PEWTER IS

distinct fragments of the lid of a tea-pot of eighteenth-century Japanese pewter he found that one portion contained 80.48 per cent. of tin to 20.02 of lead, while the other showed 77.64 per cent. of tin and 22.5 of lead, though there was no reason to suppose that the material was not originally, when in a state of fusion, perfectly homogeneous. The cause of this curious inconsistency in the results was fully explained at the same time. " Professor Brown-Austen," to quote the Abstract of the discussion given in the Journal of the Society, " had shown by means of the thermo-electric pyrometer, that when an alloy was in the act of cooling, several definite alloys, in which the molecules of the metals were differently grouped from those of the mass, fell out at definite temperatures, so that the solidified metal did not consist really of one alloy, but was a mixture of several, more or less regularly diffused throughout the mass," the margin of possible error from this cause, according to Mr. Gowland, averaging about 2 per cent. for small vessels which would cool quickly and fairly uniformly, and as much as 4 per cent. in larger vessels.

It follows from this that since no collector

is likely to sacrifice an entire object for the purpose of ascertaining its composition with scientific precision, the quality of any given specimen of pewter can only be arrived at in a rough-and-ready fashion. Excess of lead is revealed by the weight and the dark colour of the surface, and the proportion may be discovered approximately, according to Mr. Massé, by the degree to which it is possible to make a mark on paper with the metal. Pure lead leaves a dark mark like a pencil, pure tin makes none, nor does an alloy which contains more than three parts of tin to one of lead. This combination just leaves a faint trace, and the darker the mark appears the more lead and the less tin has been used in the alloy. Pure tin again, owing to its peculiar crystalline structure, gives out a characteristic sound when scratched with a knife, and an equally remarkable and unmistakable crackle or "cri" when bent, while lead gives no such response. The nature of the sound produced may therefore serve as a vague criterion of the goodness of the pewter, but this test, Mr. Massé observes, is only trustworthy to a very limited extent, since the addition of a very small amount of zinc to the purest tin

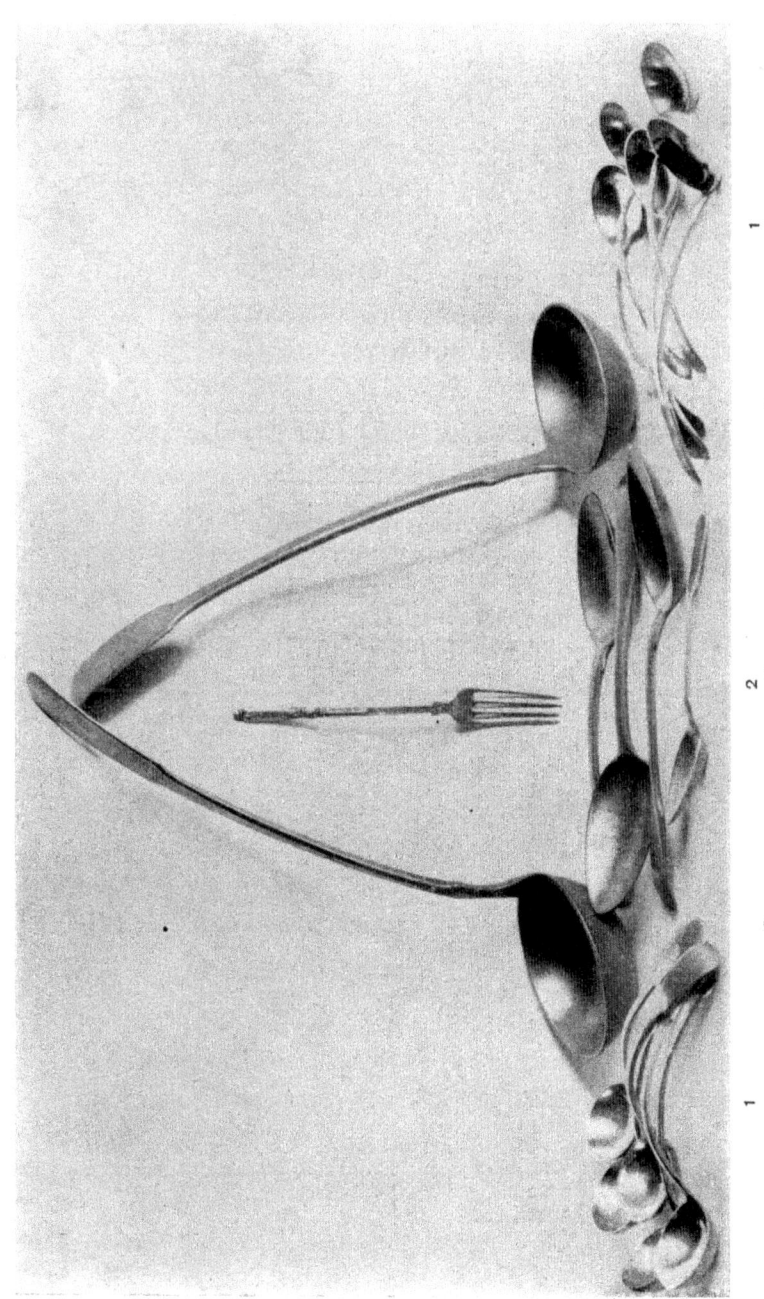

For Descriptions, see back of Plate.

DESCRIPTIONS OF OBJECTS ON PLATE XI.

1. Toddy Ladles, marked John Yates. VR crowned.
2. Small fork, no mark. Length 7″.
3. Soup ladle, marked [JO] [HN] [YA] [TES]
4. Soup ladle, marked [ASK] [BER] [RY]
   W. crown. R.
   BEST METAL
   WARRANTED
   FOR USE
5. Three table spoon, marked

   [JO] [HN] [VA] [TES] VR crowned.
6. Tea spoon, marked A1
   W
   Crowned head
   K
   PURE

WHAT PEWTER IS

at once destroys the tendency to emit the "crackle." Lastly, a rule of thumb test employed in former days by French pewterers consisted in touching the metal with a hot iron and judging the quality by the whiteness of the scar which resulted on good pewter, or the increasing depth of the brown observable as the stuff deteriorated.

The question, after all, is for the collector mainly an academic one of little practical importance. When the purchaser was buying for domestic use, and in especial when he proposed to store in it wine, vinegar, or any other liquid of which the natural acidity might act on any excess of lead, giving rise to actively poisonous chemical compounds, it was a matter of great moment, but such a preponderance in no way affects the artistic or historical value of the specimen, and as none of the metals that may be present has, speaking broadly, much intrinsic worth, its money value is in no way dependent upon the character of the material.

In case, however, any owner of pewter should be desirous of ascertaining with some degree of certainty the composition of any article in his possession, a fairly simple method of procedure is here appended. Scrape from some inconspicuous portion of the vessel sufficient material, taking due care that the instrument used is scrupulously clean, as, indeed, must be the case with all the apparatus employed, and endeavouring, if convenient, for the reason given above, to secure a number of small fragments from different parts of the surface rather than a larger scraping from one only. If the subsequent operations are conducted with great care and a delicate balance is used, from three to four grams weight, or about an eighth of an ounce, should be enough, though it is needless to say that every increase in the portion experimented upon will diminish the liability to error by facilitating the task of weighing the constituents later on. Weigh the scraps of metal so obtained carefully in an accurate balance, place them in a glass flask or other convenient vessel, and pour upon them a mixture of strong nitric acid diluted with half its volume of water. The action of the acid on the metal will be at once observable by a brisk effervescence, and as soon as this appears to be slackening gently warm the flask. When it is finished a fine white

DESCRIPTIONS OF OBJECTS ON PLATE XII.

THE MAKERS' MARKS, WHERE LEGIBLE, ARE
SHOWN ON PLATE CIV.

1. Laton spoon, 5″ long, found in the Thames at Westminster; an engraved line runs along lower surface of stem. XIV century.
2. Bronze spoon, 6¾″ long, found in the city of London. XIV century. Probably French.
3. Laton spoon, 6″ long, French. XIV century.
4. Laton spoon, 6¾″ long, found in the Thames in London, stem of diamond section. Early XV century.
5. Laton spoon, 7″ long, found in London. Early 15 century. Probably French.
6. Bronze spoon, 5¾″ long, found in London, XV century.
7. Bronze spoon, 6″ long, stem of diamond section, found in London. XV century.
8. Bronze spoon, 6⅛″ long, found in London. XV century. Mark same as No. 2.

PLATE XII

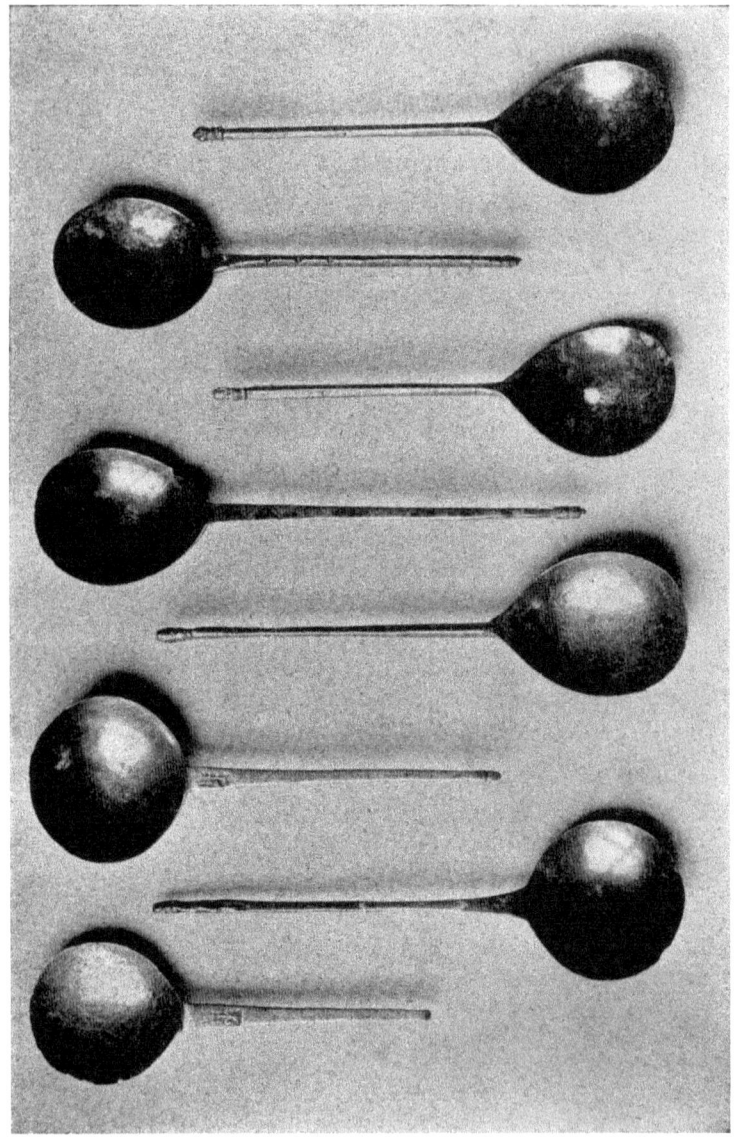

For Descriptions, see back of Plate.

WHAT PEWTER IS

powder or precipitate will be visible suspended in the otherwise clear liquid. That is all the tin present, now in the form of oxide. Next dilute the liquid in the flask with about three times its volume of water and heat it, keeping it meanwhile in a constant state of agitation. Then leave the precipitate to settle, and when that is done pour off the liquid carefully into another vessel, taking care that all the oxide remains behind. Preserve the liquid poured off, as that still holds in solution the remaining constituents of the alloy. To the small residuum containing the precipitate add more nitric acid, diluted with about six times its volume of water, and heat again. Pass it then through a chemist's filter-paper properly folded in a glass funnel, and when the dilute acid has all run through pour water on the powder on the filter-paper so as to wash it thoroughly. If the water on coming from the filter is at all blue in colour copper is still being dissolved, and the treatment with the second or weaker dilution of nitric acid must be repeated until on washing as before no shade of blue can be detected. All the liquid that has passed through the filter should be added to that

OLD PEWTER

which was first poured off and reserved for further treatment. The filter-paper, with the powder adhering to it, must be dried thoroughly in a small porcelain crucible, and when that is done the paper lighted and left to burn to ashes, which will be so infinitesimal in weight as not to affect materially the result. Heat the remnant over a Bunsen burner, or spirit lamp, and keep it for a time at a dull red glow to drive off any water remaining free or in combination, and when it has cooled weigh carefully; 75 parts of oxide of tin contain 59 parts of pure metallic tin, so that if the result be multiplied by 59 and divided by 75 you will have the exact weight of pure tin in the alloy and can easily calculate the percentage.

The next step is to release the lead. Into the liquid which has been previously set aside pour a small quantity of strong sulphuric acid and evaporate it down in a glass or porcelain basin, taking care that it does not boil with sufficient violence to spurt over the edge, until it begins to give off thick white fumes. This operation drives off the nitric acid which is no longer useful. Now dilute the liquid with water and again a cloud of

DESCRIPTIONS OF OBJECTS ON PLATE XIII.

THE MAKERS' MARKS, WHERE LEGIBLE, ARE SHOWN ON PLATE CIV.

1. Pewter slip-top spoon, $6\frac{1}{2}''$ long, found at Bermondsey, stem of hexagonal section. XVI century.
2. Pewter slip-top spoon, $6\frac{1}{2}''$ long, found in London. XVI century.
3. Pewter slip-top spoon, $6\frac{3}{4}''$ long. XVI century.
4. Pewter slip-top spoon, $6\frac{1}{2}''$ long. XVII century.
5. Pewter slip-top spoon, $6\frac{3}{4}''$ long, found in London. XVI century.
6. Pewter slip-top spoon, $6''$ long, found in York Road, Westminster. XVI century.
7. Pewter slip-top spoon, $6\frac{1}{4}''$ long, found in London. XVI century.
8. Pewter slip-top spoon, $6\frac{1}{4}''$ long, found in London. XVII century.

PLATE XIII

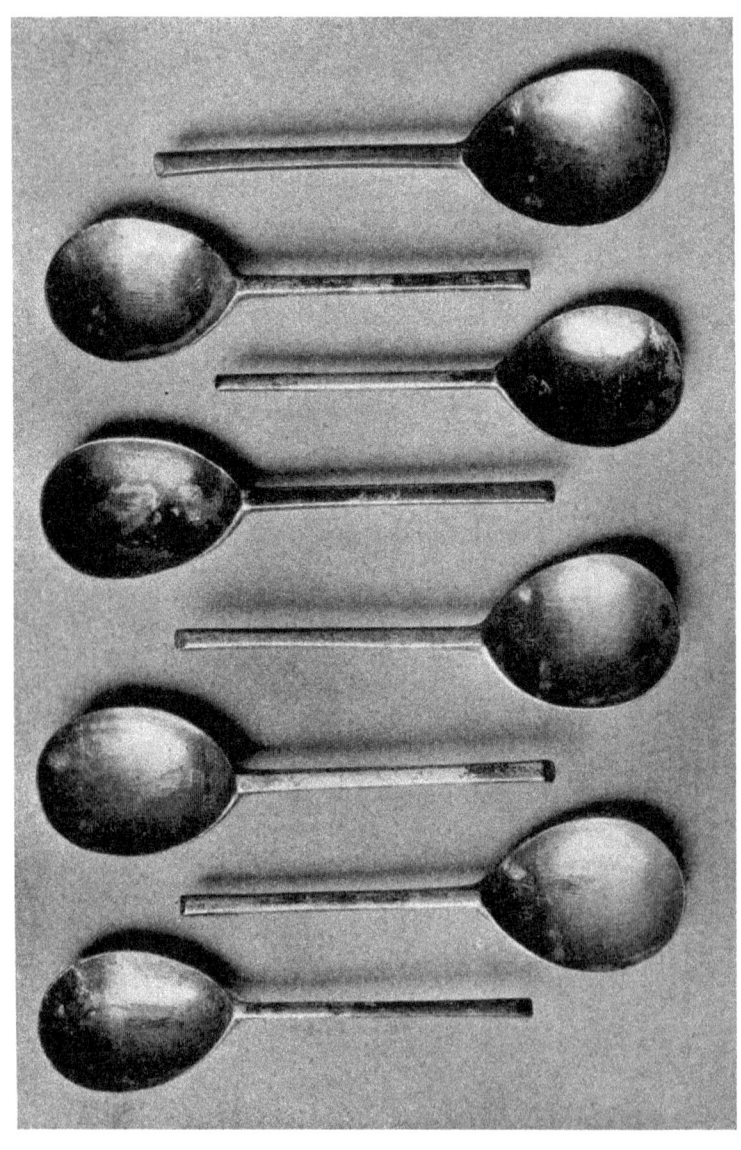

For Descriptions, see back of Plate.

PLATE XIV

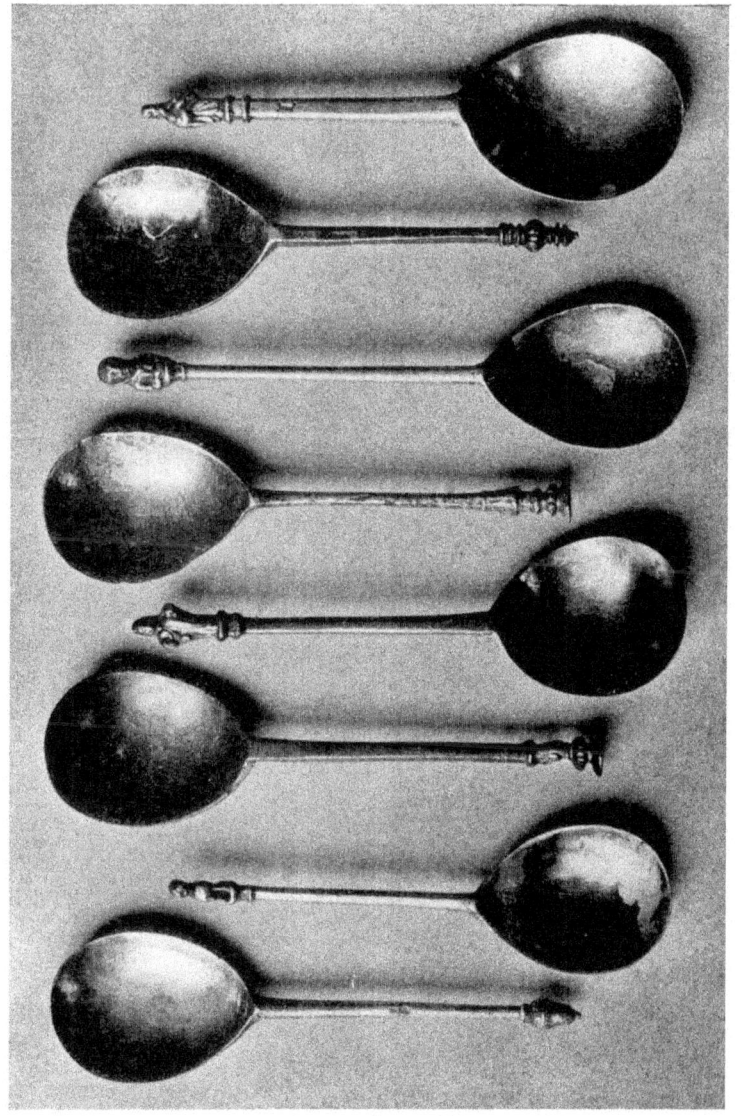

1   2   3   4   5   6   7   8
For Descriptions, see back of Plate.

DESCRIPTIONS OF OBJECTS ON PLATE XIV.

THE MAKERS' MARKS, WHERE LEGIBLE, ARE SHOWN ON PLATE CIV.

1. Pewter spoon, $6\frac{1}{2}''$ long, found in London. XVI century.
2. Pewter spoon, $6\frac{1}{4}''$ long. XVII century.
3. Laton spoon, $6\frac{3}{4}''$ long, found in London, stem of hexagonal section. XVII century.
4. Laton spoon, with Apostle top, $6\frac{1}{2}''$ long. XVII century.
5. Pewter spoon, seal headed, hexagonal, $6\frac{1}{2}''$ long, found at Bermondsey. XVI century.
6. Pewter sacramental spoon, with Maidenhead top, $7\frac{1}{4}''$ long, found in London. XVI century.
7. Pewter spoon, $6\frac{1}{2}''$ long, found in London. XVII century.
8. Pewter spoon, with Apostle top, $6\frac{3}{4}''$ long, found in London. XVI century.

WHAT PEWTER IS

fine white powder will appear. That is the lead in the form of sulphate of lead. Filter and wash as before, only adding a few drops of sulphuric acid to the water used. Once more set aside the liquid that comes through the filter, which will still hold in solution any constituents of the alloy other than tin or lead. Wash the powder in the filter with alcohol or methylated spirit, but throw this away after it is done with as it can serve no further purpose; then dry, burn off, heat awhile, and weigh as in the case of the tin oxide; 151 parts of sulphate of lead contain 103 parts of lead, and a simple calculation, as in the former case, will give the true weight of the lead and the percentage.

If the alloy contains any appreciable quantity of copper the liquid which has been reserved from the first washing will have a blue colour. To secure this copper is easy, but, within-doors at any rate, somewhat unpleasant. The first step consists in passing through the liquid sulphuretted hydrogen gas, easily made by pouring sulphuric acid on sulphite of iron in a suitable vessel, but disagreeably distinguished by possessing a powerful and highly offensive odour of rotten eggs. A fine powder, black in colour this time, will soon appear. That is the copper in the form of copper sulphide. Repeat with this the now familiar operations of filtering and washing. It is then redissolved in dilute nitric acid and a solution of caustic potash (potassium hydrate) is added. The precipitate reappears in the form of copper oxide, which may then be filtered out, dried, burnt off, and so on previous to weighing; 159 parts of copper oxide contain 127 parts of copper.

The final test for zinc is easy. A solution of sodium carbonate added to the remaining liquid will at once precipitate it as zinc oxide. This should be white, but will possibly be more or less tinged with reddish brown, a proof that a slight accidental impurity is present in the form of iron, which, however, may be ignored. The washing, filtering, &c., are next carried out, but the final heating to drive off the water must be done with great care, as zinc evaporates at a comparatively low temperature, and floating off as a gas will be lost; 81 parts of zinc oxide contain 65 parts of zinc.

In some kinds of pewter, as has been

PLATE XV

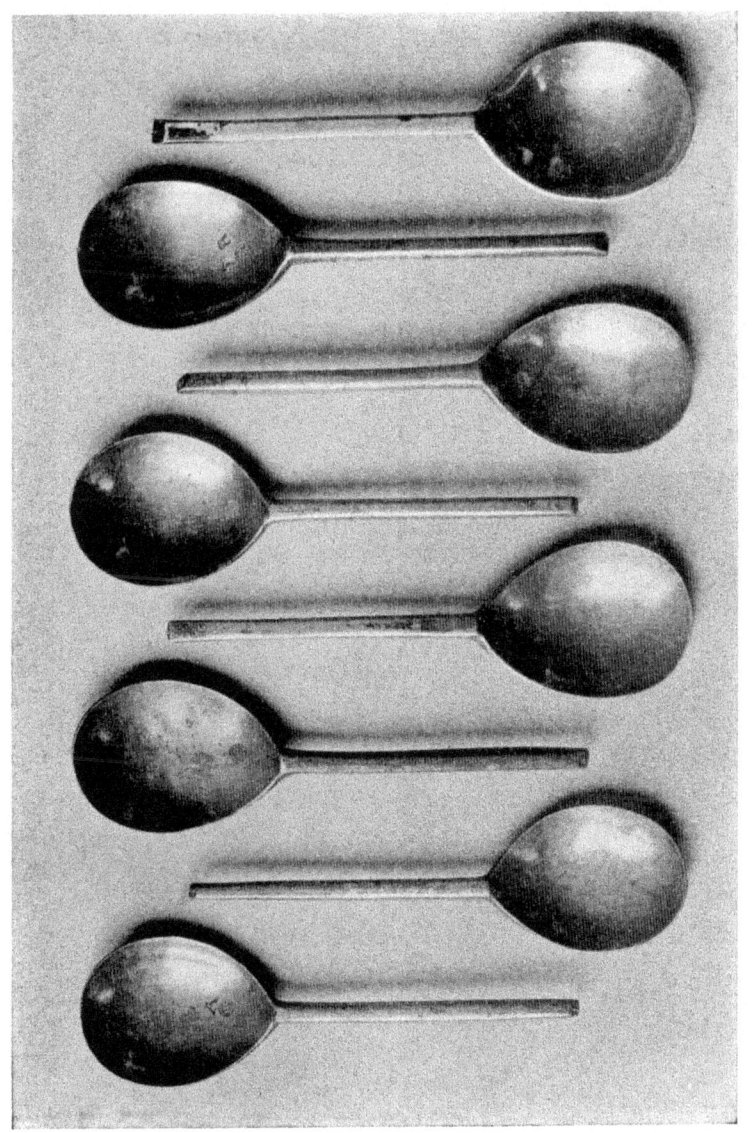

For Descriptions, see back of Plate.

DESCRIPTIONS OF OBJECTS ON PLATE XV.

THE MAKERS' MARKS, WHERE LEGIBLE, ARE SHOWN ON PLATE CV.

1. Pewter slip-top spoon, 6″ long, found in York Road, Westminster. XVI century. Same mark as Plate XIII, Fig. 6.
2. Pewter slip-top spoon, 6″ long, found in London. XVI century. Same mark as plate XIII, Fig. 6.
3. The same as Fig. 2.
4. Pewter slip-top spoon, 6½″ long, found in London. XVI century.
5. Pewter slip-top spoon, 6¼″ long. XVI century.
6. Pewter slip-top spoon, 6½″ long, found in London. XVI century. Same mark as Fig. 2.
7. Pewter slip-top spoon, 6½″ long. XVI century.
8. Pewter slip-top spoon, 6¾″ long, found in Bermondsey. XVI century.

WHAT PEWTER IS

previously pointed out, antimony is employed, but the separation of this is a tiresome and difficult task, only possible to a trained analytical chemist. Its presence, however, may possibly be deduced in the process of securing the copper from the orange tinge which its sulphide, in sufficient quantities, would impart to the black precipitate.

As these directions are intended solely for those unaccustomed to chemical operations, it may not perhaps be impertinent, in conclusion, to call attention to the fact that the acids used are not only virulently poisonous but distinctly deleterious in outward application to hands, clothes, tablecloths, &c., and should consequently be handled with ample caution, and either thrown away at once or carefully locked up when done with.

THE THIRD CHAPTER
HOW PEWTER WAS WROUGHT

URING the Middle Ages, when the now nearly extinct craft of the pewterer was in the heyday of its prosperity, the actions of its followers were circumscribed, their every proceeding regulated, and their offences against the rules and ordinances from time to time established punished with a rigour and ruthlessness unequalled even by the tyrannous edicts of modern Trades Unions. Unlike these last, however, the laws were made not solely for the benefit of the so-called working man but for the general good. The cynical doctrine, *caveat emptor*, found no adherents in those days. The rules of the Company were not indeed wholly unconcerned with the welfare of the craft and craftsmen, some of them in fact display a very sufficient amount of greed and selfishness, but they did not set on one side as useless or even harmful its good name and honour. The modern idea would seem to be that no man, however skilful, however diligent, shall be permitted

DESCRIPTIONS OF OBJECTS ON PLATE XVI.

THE MAKERS' MARKS, WHERE LEGIBLE, ARE
SHOWN ON PLATE CV.

1. Pewter slip-top spoon, $6\frac{3}{4}''$ long, found at Bermondsey. XVI century.
2. Pewter slip-top spoon, $7\frac{1}{4}''$ long, found in London. XVI century.
3. Pewter slip-top spoon, $6\frac{3}{4}''$ long, found at Bermondsey. XVI century.
4. Pewter slip-top spoon, $6\frac{1}{2}''$ long, found at Bermondsey. XVI century.
5. Laton slip-top spoon, $6\frac{1}{4}''$ long, found at Bermondsey, has remains of tin plating. XVII century.
6. Laton slip-top spoon, $7''$ long, found at Bermondsey. XVII century.
7. Laton slip-top spoon, $6\frac{3}{16}''$ long, found in London, has remains of tin plating. XVII century.
8. Pewter slip-top spoon, $6\frac{1}{2}''$ long, found in London. XVI century.
9. Pewter slip-top spoon, $6\frac{3}{4}''$ long, found in London. XVI century.

PLATE XVI

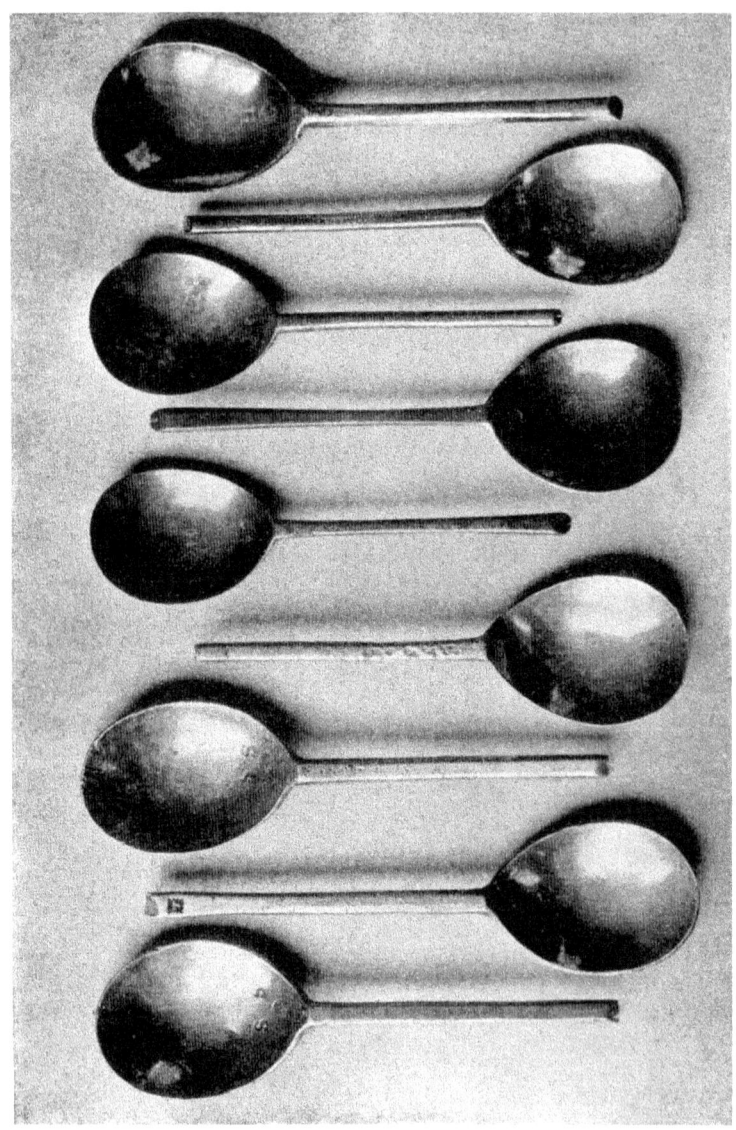

For Descriptions, see back of Plate.

HOW PEWTER WAS WROUGHT

to turn out more work or better work than the most sluggish and incompetent can produce in the same time. The old notion was that no man should be allowed to foist upon an innocent public work below a certain definite standard of merit, while any and every man should be encouraged to advance as far beyond that standard as in him lay. It was recognised that it was not only to the credit but to the interest of the craft as a whole to deal honestly with the customer and to make sure that he was given exactly what he expected and had a right to, not the omnipresent " just as good " of nowadays, which in the majority of cases means infinitely worse. How, when, and where the vessel was made, its weight, quality, and price, by whom, to whom, and in what places it was sold, were all elaborately provided for, and woe betide the knave or fool who made or dealt otherwise. The first conviction for illegal practices was followed by the confiscation of the inferior object or material, and the second confiscation was supplemented by " punishment at the discretion of the Mayor and Aldermen," while a third resulted in expulsion from the craft, which in those days of closely guarded Guilds must have meant in most instances starvation or the gallows.

The Company did not, moreover, confine itself to simply ordering the craftsman as trader, but interfered most minutely with nearly every detail of his daily life. With these domestic and social restraints, curious and often amusing as they are, we cannot here concern ourselves. The reader who would learn more may be confidently referred to Mr. Welch's exhaustive "History of the Pewterers' Company," and Mr. Ingleby Wood's no less excellent "Scottish Pewter Ware and Pewterers." We must content ourselves with summarising the general trend of the regulations governing the trade, without laying stress upon the minor differences which prevailed in different places.

Before the master-pewterer could set up in business for himself he had to go through a long apprenticeship, as a rule six years, with an added year during which the work done by the then fully trained craftsman was supposed to repay his master for the cost he had incurred, and no master was allowed to be so "daring as to receive any workman of the craft if he have not been an apprentice." When this

PLATE XVII

1 2 3 4 5 6 7 8

For Descriptions, see back of Plate.

DESCRIPTIONS OF OBJECTS ON PLATE XVII.

THE MAKERS' MARKS, WHERE LEGIBLE, ARE SHOWN ON PLATE CV.

1. Laton seal-top spoon, $5\frac{3}{4}''$ long, found in London. XVII century.
2. Laton seal-top spoon, $6\frac{1}{2}''$ long. XVII century.
3. Laton seal-top spoon, $6\frac{3}{4}''$ long. XVII century.
4. Laton seal-top spoon, $6\frac{1}{4}''$ long, found in London. XVII century.
5. Laton seal-top spoon, $6\frac{3}{16}''$ long, found in London. XVII century.
6. Laton seal-top spoon, $6\frac{1}{2}''$ long, found in London. XVII century.
7. Laton seal-top spoon, $6\frac{1}{8}''$ long, found in London. XVII century.
8. Laton seal-top spoon, $6\frac{1}{8}''$ long, found in London. XVII century.

HOW PEWTER WAS WROUGHT

time of probation was out he was expected to produce under test conditions his "essay," certain prescribed vessels which differed in nature at different times and places, and only when these had been submitted to and approved by the authorities of the craft was he allowed to take up his "freedom," register his private "touch" on the proper plate at the Company's Hall, and set up in business for himself. It was only to the native-born, however, that even these preliminary steps were open; they had no altruistic sentimentality in those days, being fully determined to keep their trade and its secrets to themselves as far as possible, and to that end fining any master employing a foreigner ten pounds besides confiscating any ware made by him. The apprentice doubtless began with the merely mechanical part of the work, advancing by degrees to such simple matters as the making of spoons, a despised task relegated to the young or the infirm, and gradually progressing to more important objects as he gained skill in the particular branch he practised. These in England were three—Sadware men, Hollow-ware men and Triflers, corresponding fairly closely with the French sub-divisions, *Potiers maîtres de*

OLD PEWTER

forge, Potiers dit de rond, and *Potiers menuisiers*. The Sadware men, who were not rated very highly in the craft, made dishes, trenchers, chargers, and other more or less flat and open vessels of weight. The derivation and significance of the term are doubtful, and it is perhaps more ingenious than allowable to refer it to the original meaning of sad, as given by Professor Skeat, namely " satiated," and to attribute its use in this connection to the fact that the material used by the members of this branch was that " fine pewter " which, as explained in the last chapter, consisted of tin alloyed with as much copper as " of its own nature it will take," in other words, satiated, or as chemists would say, saturated. This conjecture, far-fetched as it may appear, is to some extent supported by the circumstance that the third branch, the Triflers, were indisputably so called because they worked in the mixture of 82 or 83 parts of tin to 18 or 17 of antimony, known as "trifle." The term Hollow-ware men sufficiently explains itself as denoting the nature of the object produced, not the material of which it was fashioned.

Whichever of these three branches of the

DESCRIPTIONS OF OBJECTS ON PLATE XVIII.

THE MAKERS' MARKS, WHERE LEGIBLE, ARE SHOWN ON PLATE CVI.

1. Laton slip-top spoon, $7\frac{3}{4}''$ long, plated with tin, found in London. XVII century.
2. Pewter slip-top spoon, $7''$ long, found at Bermondsey. XVII century.
3. Laton slip-top spoon, $6\frac{1}{4}''$ long, found in London. XVII century.
4. Laton spoon, $7\frac{1}{4}''$ long, plated with tin. XVII century.
5. Laton spoon, $5\frac{3}{4}''$ long, with remains of tin plating. XVII century.
6. Laton spoon, $7\frac{1}{4}''$ long, plated with tin. Handle "Pied de Biche." Mark same as Fig. 5.
7. Laton spoon, $7\frac{1}{8}''$ long, with remains of tin plating. Handle "Pied de Biche." XVII century.
8. Laton rat-tailed spoon, $7\frac{1}{4}''$ long, found in York Road, Westminster. Handle "Pied de Biche." XVII century.

PLATE XVIII

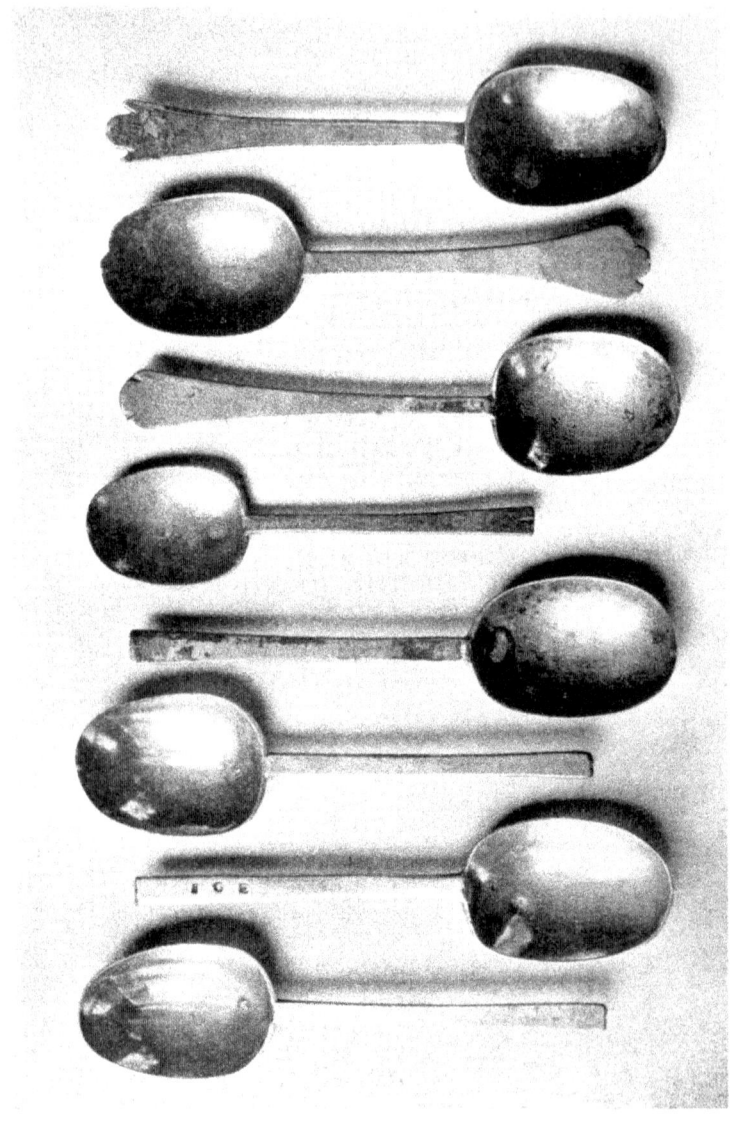

For Descriptions, see back of Plate.

PLATE XIX

1 2 3 4 5 6 7 8 9

For Descriptions, see back of Plate.

DESCRIPTIONS OF OBJECTS ON PLATE XIX.

THE MAKERS' MARKS, WHERE LEGIBLE, ARE SHOWN ON PLATE CVI.

1. Laton rat-tailed spoon, 8" long, plated with tin. Handle "Pied de Biche." XVII century.
2. Pewter rat-tailed spoon, $7\frac{1}{4}$" long, found in Newgate Street. Handle "Pied de Biche." XVII century.
3. Laton rat-tailed spoon, 7" long, found in York Road, Westminster, plated with tin. XVII century.
4. Pewter rat-tailed spoon, $7\frac{3}{4}$" long, found in Bermondsey. XVII century.
5. Pewter rat-tailed spoon, $7\frac{3}{4}$" long, found in Bermondsey. XVII century.
6. Pewter rat-tailed spoon, 7" long. XVII century.
7. Laton spoon, $5\frac{7}{8}$" long, plated with pewter, found in London. Late XVII century.
8. Bronze rat-tailed spoon, $5\frac{3}{4}$" long. XVII century.
9. Rat-tailed pewter chocolate spoon, 4" long, found in the Wandle at Wandsworth. XVII century.

HOW PEWTER WAS WROUGHT

trade he followed, the worker's first business must have been to make his alloy, mixing his tin and lead or copper in the ordained proportions, with a careful eye on the "sharp laws provided in that behalf" mentioned by Harrison. At any moment the searchers authorised by the Master and Wardens of the Company might swoop down upon him and demand to assay the work he was engaged upon or had already completed for sale, and any serious deviation from the standard meant fine and confiscation of the ley, lea, or lay metal, as the debased material was called. That he might not, however, be punished for a fault that was none of his own, the Company were empowered to assay all tin on its arrival in London, and thereby to shut out "the multitude of tin which was untrue and deceyvable brought to the City, the defaults not being perceptible until it comes to the melting." Of this guaranteed tin it was customary to cast a disk, keeping the mould so that in any case of doubt a similar disk of the questionable alloy might be cast in it, when, the weights of tin and lead or copper respectively being known, the calculation of the quantity of each present was easily made.

OLD PEWTER

The tin came from Cornwall, the Warden of the Company having the legal right to purchase at the market price one-fourth of all that came into the market, retailing it at a small profit to the freemen, and it was to the superior quality of the metal there obtained that English pewter owed its high reputation in foreign lands. The birth of this industry is hidden in the mists of remote antiquity, for as an element in bronze the use of the metal goes back to dim pre-historic times. In the Book of Numbers, xxxi. 22, it is included with "the gold, and the silver, the brass, the iron, and the lead" among the spoils "that may abide the fire" which were ordered by Moses to be made to "go through the fire" for purposes of purification after the victory over the Midianites. Isaiah, i. 25, mentions it metaphorically : "I will turn my hand upon thee, and purely purge away thy dross, and take away all thy tin"; and Ezekiel, in the same style, xxii. 18 and 20, says, "The house of Israel has become to me as dross; all they are brass, and tin, and iron, and lead in the midst of the furnace"; and, "as they gather silver, and brass, and iron, and lead, and tin into the midst of the furnace, to blow the fire

DESCRIPTIONS OF OBJECTS ON PLATE XX.

THE MAKERS' MARKS, WHERE LEGIBLE, ARE
SHOWN ON PLATE CVI.

1. Pewter spoon, 8½″ long, found in London. Late XVIII century.
2. Laton dog-nose gravy spoon, 10¾″ long, plated with tin. XVII century.
3. Pewter spoon, 7¾″ long, found in Bermondsey. Late XVIII century.
4. Laton slip-top ladle, 8¾″ long, the handle of hexagonal section. XVII century.
5. Laton slip-top ladle, 8″ long, found in the city of London, has remains of tin plating. XVII century.
6. Laton slip-top ladle, 7¼″ long, found in Suffolk. XVII century.
7. Laton slip-top ladle, 6½″ long, found in London. XVII century.
8. Laton spoon, seal-headed, 6½″ long, has remains of tin plating, found at Norwich. XVII century.

PLATE XX

For Descriptions, see back of Plate.

HOW PEWTER WAS WROUGHT

upon it to melt it, so will I gather you in mine anger and in my fury; and I will leave you there and melt you," while in the recital of the various markets (xxvii. 12) contributing to the splendours of Tarsus, which precedes the prophecy of its downfall, he states that "Tarshish was thy merchant by reason of the multitude of all kinds of riches; with silver, iron, tin, and lead they traded in thy fairs." It is not probable that this tin which was brought in by the merchants of Tarshish came in the ships of Phœnician or Carthaginian seamen from these little islands in the far-away northern seas, for Tarshish has been plausibly identified with Tartessus, a port in the south of Spain, which country is known to have produced tin at one time, and Ezekiel certainly wrote centuries before Herodotus, who did undoubtedly refer to them as the Cassiterides, from the Greek word κασσίτερος, which is made use of by Homer also, and other Greek writers. Tin, "plumbum candidum," as Pliny calls it, in contradistinction to lead, "plumbum nigrum," is frequently referred to by Roman authors, and was very extensively imported in their days from England to the Continent in the form of small dice-like cubes, being embarked at Ictis, an uncertain locality believed by various differing authorities to be St. Michael's Mount, Falmouth, Weymouth, and the Isle of Wight, and delivered for distribution at Marseilles in Roman days; later principally at Bruges. All the other metals employed were also home products, antimony in the form of sulphide (stibnite), bismuth, copper, zinc in the form of zinc-blende, and lead being all found in Cornwall, though most of the last, at any rate, originally came apparently from Derbyshire, if we may form any conclusion from the fact that it was known as "Peak" to the London workers.

The alloy once duly compounded according to law, or bought ready mixed—as was evidently sometimes the case since it was forbidden to buy it by night, in other words clandestinely, or from tilers, labourers, boys, or women! all of whom were presumably expected to have stolen it, or to sell old pewter as new, such when bought being obligatorily melted down and recast—its subsequent treatment depended on the article into which it was to be converted and the class of workmen using it. For making the largest dishes and

PLATE XXI

1
PYX, hexagonal. English. XIV century.

2 H. 13″
COMMUNION FLAGON, English, from Midhurst Church, Sussex, 1677.

3
CHALICE AND PATEN, from Kriswick.

PLATE XXII

1 H. 12¾"	2 D. 10¼"	3 D. 4¼" 3
COMMUNION FLAGON, English. XVII century.	ALMS DISH. Scotch. XVIII century. Marked AS. IK.	PATENS from a Church in Yorkshire. English. XV century.

HOW PEWTER WAS WROUGHT

chargers it was rolled into a sheet, and the Sadware man was then compelled to fashion it entirely by hammering, a process which consolidated the metal and gave the necessary rigidity while at the same time producing the desirable smoothness of surface. Smaller plates and dishes and all other articles were cast. The moulds for this purpose were usually made of gun-metal finished with precise care, and as these were consequently expensive it was often the custom for the Company to own them in common, each member taking his turn in borrowing one or another as he required it, giving proper notice to the Company when he was about to make castings in order that a searcher might attend to make sure that only good metal was used.

Several lists of the various forms of these have been preserved, the earliest of which, as recorded by Mr. Welch, dating from 1425, is as follows: " 1 holow scharyder," 1 C platmolde, 1 C dysche molde, 1 C sawsyrmolde, 1 medyll plat molde, 1 medyll dysche molde, 1 medyll sawsyr molde, 1 kyngs ys dysche molde, 1 holow dysche molde, 1 holow sawsyr molde, 1 saly dysche molde, 1 saly sawsyr molde, 1 salū bolle molde, 1 qware bolle molde,

1 trechor molde." Some of these terms are of very doubtful import, but a comparison of this list with one of the regulation weights for various articles as laid down in 1430, making due allowance for the eccentricity of spelling at the time, suggests that they were a mould for hollow chargers, each of which had to weigh $2\frac{3}{4}$ pounds (the larger ones, weighing respectively 7, 5 and $3\frac{1}{4}$ pounds, were hammered); large, middle, and hollow plate, dish, and saucer moulds, weighing, for the first $2\frac{1}{2}$, 2 and $1\frac{5}{6}$ pounds each, for the second $1\frac{1}{2}$, $1\frac{1}{6}$ and 1 pound each, and for the third $\frac{3}{4}$, $\frac{7}{12}$ and $\frac{1}{3}$ of a pound each; and a mould for king's dishes, each of which weighed $1\frac{1}{3}$ pounds The saly dish, saucer, and bowl would seem to correspond with the galley dishes and saucers of the second list, weighing either 1 pound or $\frac{6}{7}$ of a pound each, which perhaps were equivalent to the "flat, cowped, and squard saler" of the York regulations of 1419, the "12 sallite" dishes in an inventory of Sir William Fairfax's possessions at Gilling drawn up in 1564, and Sir Richard Poullett's "14 small sallet pewter dishes" in an inventory of 1618. The meaning of a qware bowl is hard to guess, for the obvious suggestion,

PLATE XXIII

H. 13¼"
CHURCH FLAGON, Scotch. Early XVIII century type.

HOW PEWTER WAS WROUGHT

square, seems highly hazardous, and the supposition that "trechor" is simply trencher misspelt is scarcely less so. This collection of moulds, however, was far from complete, for the regulations as to weight include also a middle charger weighing $3\frac{1}{4}$ pounds, a second sized platter weighing $2\frac{1}{4}$ pounds, a hollow dish weighing $1\frac{1}{2}$ of a pound, a small hollow dish weighing $\frac{5}{6}$ of a pound, a Cardinal's hatte, saucers weighing 15 pounds the dozen, Florentine dishes and saucers (greatest size) weighing 13 pounds the dozen, next size of the same weighing 12 pounds, and "small bolles" 13 pounds the dozen. The weights and fashions seem also to have been modified as time went on, for in a further list of York moulds drawn up two hundred years later we find such new names as "least dubler," "brod border dish," "unmouldishe," and "banquitin dish," while the smaller chargers then weighed 4 and 3 pounds, the smallest dish $\frac{3}{4}$ of a pound, the largest platter 3 pounds, and the smallest 1 pound. The mould, whatever its name or shape, was first coated inside with fine pumice powder, sandarach, a resinous body obtained from a small coniferous tree, *Callitris quadrivalvis*, native in North-West

OLD PEWTER

Africa, or white of egg and red ochre, and having been securely closed if made in two pieces, or properly fitted together if in more, was filled directly with the molten metal and left to cool. When taken out the surface has a singular and somewhat unpleasing colour and texture, and this had to be removed, which was effected in various ways. Sadware and spoons which were cast in one piece had to be hammered and burnished, and any attempt to save time and labour at the expense of strength by the use of a lathe was sternly repressed, while in 1686 an ingenious spoon-maker named Burton was only grudgingly permitted to employ an "engine" which, probably by stamping them, turned out spoons of good quality, on condition that he did not take advantage of the lesser cost of his process by selling his goods under the market price, at that time six shillings a gross in the country and four shillings in London.

The finishing of hollow-ware was generally a much more elaborate process. These also, when possible, as in the case of porringers and other more simple forms, were cast whole, but the more elaborate pieces with curved sides, moulded rims and bases, handles, lids

HOW PEWTER WAS WROUGHT

and other accessory parts, were cast in parts which were subsequently soldered together, and the completed article turned, scraped, and burnished on a lathe. Lastly, the maker was expected to mark each vessel by stamping on it the quality mark and his own private "touch," in order that in case of any deficiency in weight or quality it might be traced to him. Failure to comply with this sensible regulation was punishable by a fine of forty shillings. A third method of working pewter was "spinning," by which the metal was pressed with a blunt steel tool into a wooden mould spun on a lathe.

The "how" of the manufacture being so minutely provided for, the "when" and the "where" were not neglected. Working at night was forbidden, on a penalty of forty pence for the first offence, eighty for the second, and the mysterious and awesome "discretion" of the Mayor and Aldermen for the third, ostensibly on the grounds that the sight was not so profitable by night or so certain as by day, or on holy days, a restriction due to the fact that this, like all other guilds, was in the beginning a partly religious body. The regulations as to the "where" were designed, as far as might be, to keep the craft in the hands of the London pewterers, for, though they had the right of search throughout England, and were empowered to assay, rigorously enough, we may be sure, all pewter imported into London from the provinces (none was admitted from abroad), they sternly condemned as "evil-disposed persons" those who, having learned their trade in the City, went "for their singular lucre into strange regions and countries" to exercise it, incidentally revealing its secrets to the "foreigner." They even claimed the right to command any English pewterers working on the Continent to return within three months and permanently establish themselves in London on pain of forfeiting their nationality and right to "the king's protection," while for the same selfish ends it was ordained that no pewterer should work in a shop open to the street, where any country pewterer passing by might spy out the process and haply profit thereby. They, at any rate, were troubled by no doubts as to the superiority of a policy of protection over free trade, and "the open door" they favoured was one that only opened one way —outwards. At the same time, be it acknow-

PLATE XXIV

1 D. 17″   ALMS-DISH, English. XVIII century.
2 H. 5¼″   CHALICE, English. XVIII century.
3 H. 8¾″   LAVER, Scotch. Late XVIII century.

PLATE XXV

1 H. 6¼
CHALICE. Italian. No marks.

2 H. 5¾
EARTHENWARE COMMUNION JUG, mounted in pewter. Mark: Angel standing holding crossed branch. Letters indistinct. Inscribed round lid.

3 H. 6¼
CHALICE. Scotch. No marks.

HOW PEWTER WAS WROUGHT

ledged, they took good heed that only honest ware should issue from it, for no ware was allowed to be sent out of the City unless it had been previously assayed.

The selling of the finished ware was as fully provided for as the making of it. All work was to be sold by the pewterer himself in his own shop, unless by special arrangement with the would-be purchaser, or was to be offered publicly at recognised fairs and markets where the searchers could inspect and test it if they thought necessary, and such pewter must be new, the re-selling of old being strictly forbidden. Table pewter was usually sold by the "garnish," according to Harrison, consisting of 12 platters, 12 dishes, and 12 saucers, and paid for by the pound, which in his time was valued at sevenpence or eightpence. Other articles were presumably sold separately, also at so much a pound, the amount being calculated from the price of tin with a small addition for the cost of working. A reversal of the rules as to selling was made in the case of hiring-out pewter, only old pewter being admissible for the latter purpose. This would seem to have been a very profitable branch of the trade, whether the goods, known as "feast-vessels," were only loaned temporarily to some one entertaining for the nonce on an exceptionally lavish scale, or were let by the year, as was not infrequently the custom. An Earl of Northumberland, for example, during the fourteenth century, is recorded as having been in the habit of hiring no less than one hundred dozen vessels, at a charge of fourpence per dozen per annum.

On the ornamentation of pewter there is no need to dwell at length. As a broad rule, indeed, it may be said that the less extraneous decoration it has the better. Good pewter should rely for its decorative effects on its structural incidents. The fineness of its lines, the elegance of its curves, its rightness of proportion, an obvious adaptation to purpose should be all-sufficient, and any essential embellishments, such as the mouldings on rims, bases, or strengthening bands, should be as simple as possible, and should manifestly display their object at a glance. The ornament should be architectural rather than sculpturesque, and this much came fittingly within the province of the maker. His wares were intended for use, and as a consequence for subsequent fairly easy and wholly efficient

HOW PEWTER WAS WROUGHT

cleansing, and such additions as complicated coats-of-arms in high relief in the middle of dish or platter, which were made in later and degenerate days, were opposed to both. Even the attempt to tamper with the natural integrity of the plain surfaces was rarely made during the best period, and still more rarely successful; and it is, indeed, at least open to question whether many, if any, of the instances that do occur of chasing, engraving, repoussé work, or other niggling supposed embellishments were the work of the pewterer himself, but were not rather the unnecessary emendations of later ignorance and lack of taste. They have in most cases an evident amateurishness and inappropriateness that seem to stamp them as often, if not always, the evil inspirations of people who did not rightly understand the characteristics of the object or appreciate its special charm. It would, perhaps, be too rash to assert dogmatically that the subtle artistic instinct which would seem to have been, almost universally, the heritage of even the humblest craftsman in those days, assured the pewterer that the texture and colour of his material had a beauty of their own which the distraction of frivolous detail would only detract from, but there can be little doubt that he fully realised that his handiwork was destined to constant and sometimes rough usage; that this in the hands of good housewives entailed constant scouring; and that in the process, with a metal so soft and easily worn away as that in which he wrought, any decoration, whether incised or in relief, would speedily be injured if not obliterated. It was a period of decadence when pewter " de belle fasson " and " fasson d'argent " became the fashion, and the elaborate salvers, basins, and ewers of Briot and Enderlein, cast in fragments and laboriously pieced together into a useless object speciously imitating silver, were inevitably the forerunners of the later gilding, painting, lacquering, inlaying, and other gross offences against the dignity of pewter, by means of which inartistic workmen, we may hope solely at the instigation of vulgar and ostentatious customers, endeavoured to disguise with frills and fripperies the humble but honest nature of their wares. It may doubtless be maintained that fundamentally neither difficulty of execution, durability of the result nor cheapness of the actual material ought to influence the judgment in the con-

PLATE XXVI

1   2 13"   3 6⅜"

CHALICES AND CHURCH FLAGON, English.

PLATE XXVII

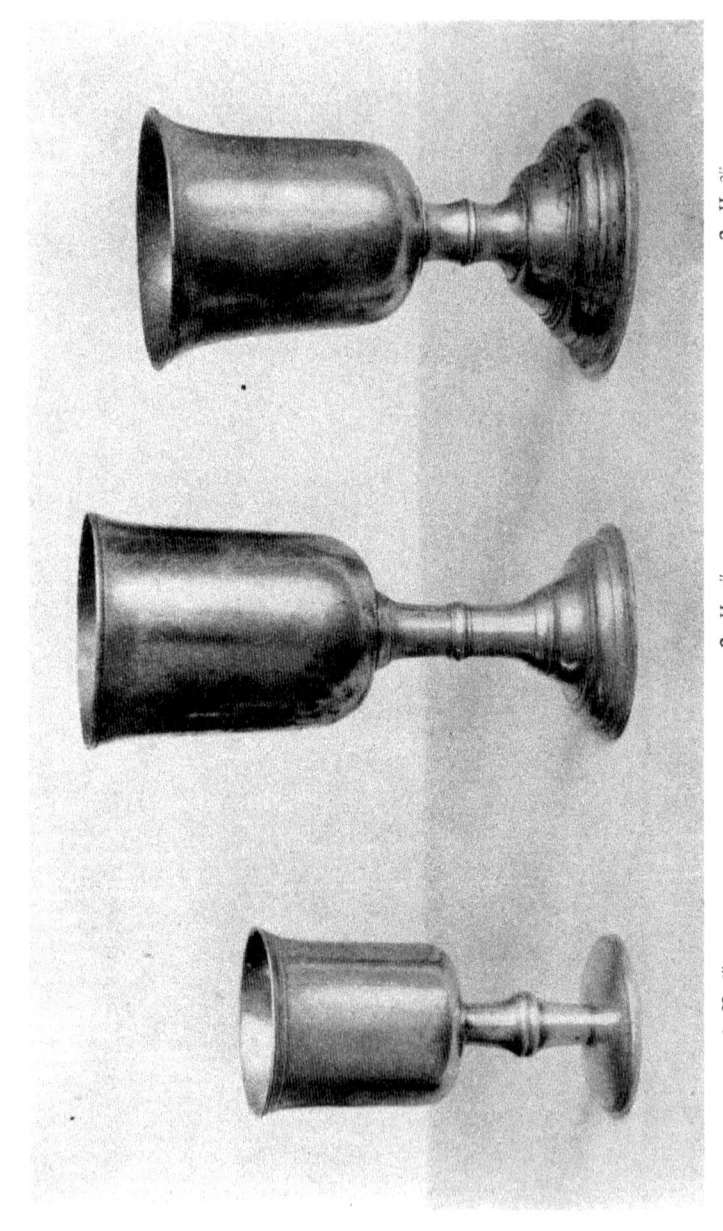

1 H. 6"   2 H. 9"   3 H. 3"

CHALICES. English. XVIII century.

HOW PEWTER WAS WROUGHT

sideration of a work of art, but one could not but doubt the sanity of a sculptor who elected to carve in crumbling sandstone when he might with equal ease obtain enduring marble, or his honesty of purpose if he painted it with white enamel to simulate it. The artist who truly respects himself and his art will not sacrifice durability to ease of manufacture, but will strive to make his work sound as well as pleasing. It is not because silver is so much more costly than pewter, but because it is of its nature so much more lasting, that the treatment which is right and proper for the one is wrong and unfit for the other. To approach in the second the effects obtainable in the first necessitates either unpardonable weakness or impracticable weight, and, at the risk of tediousness, it cannot be too often asserted that pewter fashioned in a shape that clearly prohibits usefulness is pewter misapplied.

THE FOURTH CHAPTER
SOME FACTS ABOUT PEWTER BEFORE THE FIFTEENTH CENTURY

AS with gunpowder, the mariner's compass, and other useful inventions, it seems possible that the Chinese—that strange race who advanced so far in the path of civilisation centuries ago, and then, refusing a step further, settled down into hide-bound convention—predate the Western nations in the use of pewter also, but the early history both there and here is so obscure that it is impossible to speak with any certainty. In the entire absence of all early records it is permissible to believe that the knowledge of pewter must be nearly, if not quite, as ancient as that of bronze, for it is scarcely credible that the pre-historic man who conceived the idea of mixing tin and copper and availing himself of the superior advantages of the blend to either metal by itself should have not tested also the desirability of combining the brightness, lightness, and rigidity of tin with

BEFORE FIFTEENTH CENTURY

the greater toughness and malleability of lead. This, however, in the present state of our knowledge must remain mere speculation. We first reach sure ground in the days of the Roman empire. Not only do we meet with probable references to pewter in the works of Latin writers, as in Plautus, who describes a magnificent feast served on what is generally considered to have been pewter, and in Suetonius, who states that Vitellius removed the silver vessels from the temples, replacing them with pewter, thus initiating a practice which succeeding generations followed more than once, but no inconsiderable number of pewter vessels of Roman make are still in existence. Important finds have been made in our own land at various times, chief among which ranks the remarkable collection now in the British Museum, unearthed by the Rev. R. G. Engleheart, at Appleshaw, Hampshire, in 1877, though the discoveries at Icklingham, Suffolk, in 1840, Sutton in the Isle of Ely, about 1848, Southward, Colchester and elsewhere were also notable. The Appleshaw district, which lies five miles north-west of Andover, near the intersection of the Roman roads which ran from Old Sarum to

OLD PEWTER

Silchester and from Winchester to Cirencester, had long been famous for its remains of Romano-British constructions, when in January 1897 Mr. Engleheart learned that the plough had revealed in the shape of an inscribed stone indications of yet another. The details of the building, which are fully described in *Archæologia*, vol. lvi., do not concern us here, but the pewter vessels found at the time are of unusual interest. "They appeared to be designedly hidden in a pit sunk through a cement floor, three feet below the surface of the field. The smaller vessels were carefully covered by the larger dishes." They included, as described by Mr. Charles K. Read in an appendix to the paper, ten circular dishes from twenty-two to fourteen and three-quarter inches in diameter, a square dish, fifteen and a half inches in diameter, with a semi-circular projection in the middle of each side [Plate I. 2], a chalice-shaped cup of which more anon, an octagonal jug, a portion of a circular one roughly inscribed VICTRICI, the two last letters US having been broken off, fragments of three cups, three bowls each with a curious horizontal flange round the outside, five hemi-

PLATE XXVIII

1 H. 4½″
LOVING CUP, English.

2 H. 8⅜″ D. 5⅞″
COMMUNION CUP.
Scotch.

3 D. 6¼″
PORRINGER, French.
Probably XVII century.

PLATE XXIX

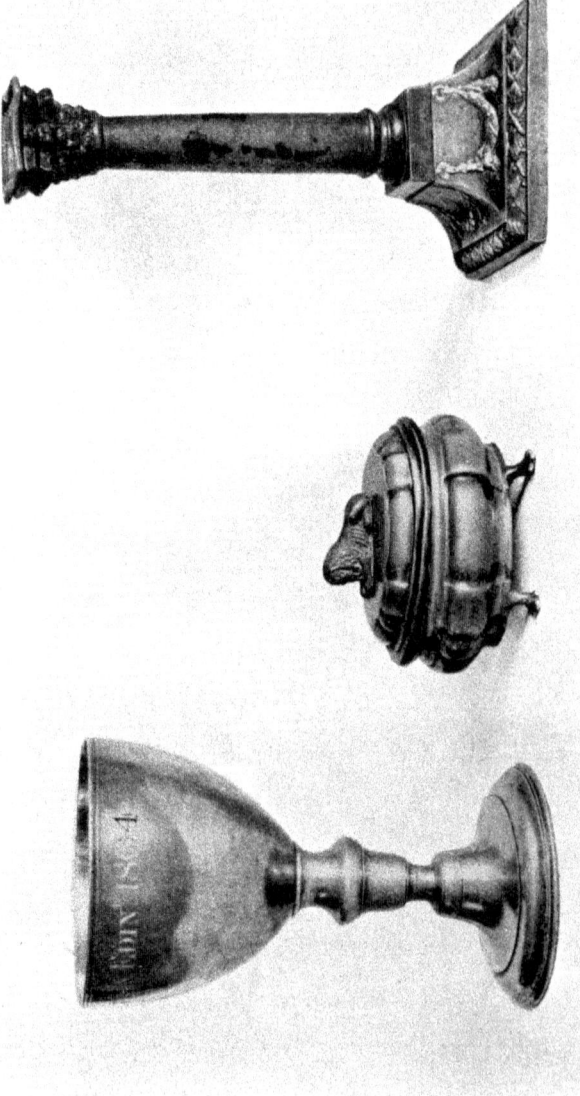

3 H. 9¼″
CANDLESTICK, French
XVIII century.

2 H. 3¾″
SPICE BOX, French.
XVIII century.

1 H. 8″
COMMUNION CUP.
1804.

BEFORE FIFTEENTH CENTURY

spherical bowls about two inches high and from six and one-eighth to four inches in diameter, two saucers, two small plates, a portion of a vase, a deep dish ten inches in diameter, and an oval dish, originally nine inches in length, of nearly pure tin. Many of them are remarkable for their ornamentation. Several of the dishes [Plate I. 1 and 3 and Plate II.] are decorated with geometrical designs of intricately interlaced strapwork produced by punching a wedge-shaped furrow afterwards filled in with a black bituminous material, not metallic as in the later Italian *niello*, which when the metal was bright must have had a highly decorative effect. The oval dish [Plate III. 3] has a fish in relief within an oval border of interlaced work, and one of the saucers [Plate III. 1] is clearly marked on the bottom with the well-known Christian symbol ☧, in connection with which two facts Mr. Engleheart, in a letter which he has kindly permitted me to quote, offers a most important suggestion: " Though I dislike guesses in archæology," he writes, " I cannot altogether dismiss a surmise of some interest which has occurred to me. In this collection of vessels we have (1) a *patera* marked, as though to distinguish it, with the Christian monogram; (2) a small dish stamped with the fish, a well-known Christian emblem, the form being almost exactly identical with the one common in the catacombs; (3) a vessel which immediately and forcibly suggests a Chalice [Plate III. 2]. Is it not at least possible that we have here a very early instance of a 'pewter communion service?' If the inmates of the villa were Christians, as would seem to be indicated by the ☧, it is highly probable that they would earmark some of their best vessels for Eucharistic use. And it is a curious concidence that a small ingot of pewter in the British Museum stamped with the ☧ is practically identical in analysis with the similarly marked *patera*," on which point Mr. Gowland speaks even more strongly, saying that " it is of precisely the same composition." Mr. Engleheart goes on to say that " C. N. Read objects to the chalice theory that the edge of the bowl is reflexed, making it difficult to drink out of. But the vessel is surely a cup. He suggests it is a lamp, but I have never seen a lamp shaped at all like this, and I have seen most of the collections of Roman ware at home and

PLATE XXX

1 H. of Chalice 2″
POCKET COMMUNION SERVICE in wooden case, bought in Iceland, probably Danish or Scotch.

2 H. 3¾″
SACRAMENTAL CRUET, Aqua, French or Flemish.

3 H. 3″
MEASURE, *temps* Charles II, found in Parliament St., Whitehall.

4 H. 4¼″
SACRAMENTAL CRUET, Vinum, French or Flemish.

PLATE XXXI

1 H. 4¾″
CRUET,
VINUM.
No marks.

2 H. 4¾″
GILL MEASURE,
Modern. Mark
V.R. Crowned.

3 H. 6¾″
HALF-
MUTCHKIN
MEASURE.
Marked.

IMPERIAL
crown
STANDARD
GLAS.   shield
51

4 H. 2⅛″
OLD
HALF
GLASS
MEASURE.
No marks.

5 H. 3″
HALF-GILL
MEASURE.
Marked like
Mutchkin;
but with two
Oval Stamps
instead of
GLAS. and
shield.

6 H. 3″
GILL
MEASURE.
No marks.

BEFORE FIFTEENTH CENTURY

abroad." When such learned doctors differ it is meet for the layman to suspend judgment. The reader may form his own conclusions from an examination of the reproduction [Plate III.]; but with regard to the objection to the chalice theory founded on the reflexed lip it may be pointed out that in a large number of surviving chalices of ancient date the lip will be seen to be more or less turned outwards in the same way.

Mr. Engleheart's supposition, if it be as correct as it is probable, has a considerable bearing on the question of the date of the objects. In his original remarks upon the find, he argued on this point as follows: "Lying on the floor, below which they were buried, was a fragment of wall-plaster bearing a peculiar pattern of red flower-buds on a white ground, absolutely identical with plaster found in the Clanville villa. Now the inscribed stone found in the latter proves that the house was inhabited in the year 234 A.D., while the coins cease with Decentius, 351 A.D. Therefore, on the not unreasonable suppositions (1) that the plaster, as found, represents the wall-decoration of the houses at the time of their destruction or abandonment; (2) that the identity of design shows a correspondence of dates; (3) that the vessels were concealed when the house was abandoned, we may assign the vessels to a period not by many years removed from 350 A.D." To which conclusion he now appends that as "the ☧ would scarcely have appeared before Constantine's sanction of Christianity in the year 311," the probable date cannot well be earlier than that. As, moreover, the Roman legions left Britain in 411 never to return, it is unlikely that they were made after that, and we may therefore feel assured that we have in them examples far more ancient than anything the Eastern world can show.

The oldest of these, indeed, to which an approximately definite date can be attributed, were some spoons seen by Mr. Gowland in the treasure-house at Nara, in Japan, among the dresses and decorations of the Court which are known to have been deposited there on the accession of the Emperor Kwammu in 784 A.D., when Kioto became the capital, a few years after the first record of the use of pewter made from tin found in the country instead of imported from China as heretofore, which innovation took place

PLATE XXXII

1 H. 24½"   2 H. 23½"   3 H. 24¼"
ALTAR CANDLESTICKS AND GERMAN GUILD CUP.
XVII century.

PLATE XXXIII

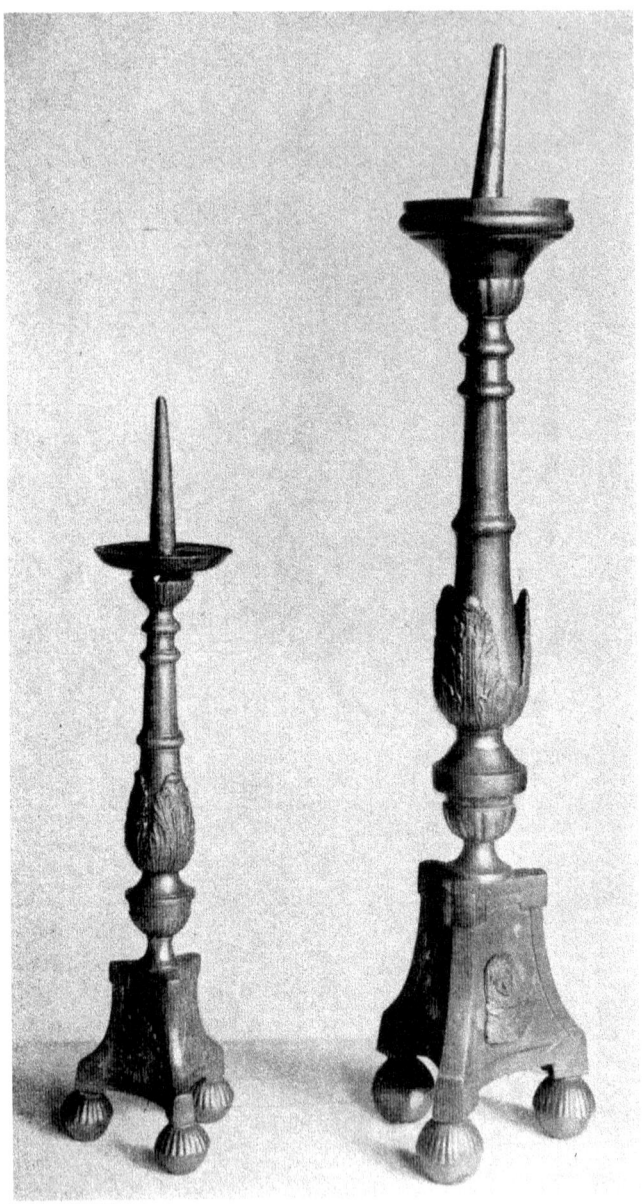

1 H 24½"   2 H 35"
ALTAR CANDLESTICKS, Flemish. XVII century.

BEFORE FIFTEENTH CENTURY

during the reign of the Empress Shokotu, which lasted from 765 A.D. to 770 A.D.

After the withdrawal of the Romans, the history of England, as in fact of all Western Europe, becomes one long tale of ceaseless wars. The hapless Britons, overmastered by the Picts and Scots, adopted the desperate remedy of calling to their help the Angles from the Jutland shores, only to find too late that in place of a trusty house-dog they had enticed into their fold a ravening wolf. Year after year, century after century, with few and brief intervals of a respite, the rashly invited invaders tightened and widened their grasp upon the land they were called in to defend, driving the natives step by step further and further westward and northward, and during the protracted struggle we may feel sure that any lingering traces of civilisation which had survived the downfall of the Roman domination were utterly swept away. How and where in Europe the memory of the peaceful arts, among them that of pewter-making, was preserved, when and where the seeds, so lying dormant, quickened again into life, we do not know. Certain it is, and that is all that is certain in the matter, that between this pewter from Appleshaw and the next objects of which we have knowledge a gap of some five or six hundred years intervened. These, consisting of rings and fibulæ of Anglo-Saxon workmanship attributed to the ninth or tenth centuries, are now in the Guildhall Museum, but are more interesting for their antiquity than for their beauty. A more important example of early post-Roman European pewter is now unhappily only known by a drawing, made in 1725 from an ornate chalice, since destroyed, of very uncertain date between the seventh and eleventh centuries, which was reproduced in the *Revue des Arts Decoratifs*, published in Paris in 1883. The first we hear of pewter, after the Latin authors already mentioned, is in connection with Church use, when, in 1074, at a Synod sitting at Rouen, wood was emphatically forbidden as a material for chalices, pewter being the only alternative admissible in those cases where the poverty of the congregation forbade the use of the more costly metals—gold or silver. An identical resolution was adopted for England by a Council held at Winchester two years later, but in the next century, at the

BEFORE FIFTEENTH CENTURY

Council of Westminster, assembled in 1175, under the presidency of Richard, Archbishop of Canterbury, pewter in its turn was degraded from its sacred offices, and the bishops were commanded not "to consecrate a pewter chalice," gold and silver being alone considered worthy. A sense of economy apparently limited this restriction to vessels made for actual Eucharistic use in the services of the Church, for the chalices which it was customary to place in the coffins of deceased churchmen to indicate their rank were still, as a rule, constructed, roughly enough, of pewter, as were the plaques sometimes added, bearing the name and title of the dead man, two of which were found at Mont St. Michel, one recording the name of Robert de Torigny, abbot from 1154 to 1186, and the other of Martin, abbot from 1186 to 1191. But stern necessity is apt to overrule the decisions even of Synods and Councils, and, as far as England was concerned, the regulation did not remain long in force, for in 1194 the sum of 10,000 marks being called for from the nation at large to pay the ransom demanded before the release of Richard Cœur de Lion, the Church plate went perforce with the rest of the kingdom's treasures into the melting-pot, and pewter was tacitly permitted to resume its erstwhile prohibited place upon the altar.

Whether the white metal alloy, of which the magnificent Gloucester candlestick [Plate IV.], now in the Victoria and Albert Museum, can in all strictness be classed as pewter, is perhaps open to dispute, but it is such a superb example of rich twelfth-century workmanship that it is not possible to pass it by without brief mention; nor need more be accorded to the grant in 1201, by King John, of charters to the Stannaries of Cornwall and Devon, which is only incidentally connected with the subject.

The exclusion of pewter from ecclesiastical use, which had so speedily fallen into abeyance in England, was soon found to be impracticable in many cases in France also, and permission to employ it had perforce to be accorded to parishes which could not afford the nobler metals by the Council of Nîmes in 1252 and confirmed by that of Albi in 1254. The first definite mention of pewter in domestic use occurs twenty years later in a record stating that the meat for the Coronation banquet of King Edward I. of England

PLATE XXXIV

W. 18"
CANDELABRUM, Flemish. XVIII century.

PLATE XXXV

D. 16¾"
ALMS DISH, German. Early XVIII century.

BEFORE FIFTEENTH CENTURY

(1274) was boiled in pewter cauldrons, and one hundred dishes, one hundred platters, and, curiously enough, more than one hundred salt-cellars formed part of the three hundred odd vessels of pewter owned by the same king in 1290. But abroad, at any rate, the popularity of pewter must have been well established long before that date, since, in his account of the Paris guilds in the middle of the thirteenth century, Etienne Boileau speaks of some twenty pewterers already differentiated into potters, nail-makers, lorimers, toy-makers, and makers of buckles and other small goods, while the pewterers of Bruges were becoming noted about the same time for their porringers and flasks.

The continued increase of its employment in this way during the succeeding years is further indicated by a rough list of Parisian craftsmen, which shows that during the eight years between 1292 and 1300 the number of makers of table vessels in wood had been reduced by eighteen and their places had been filled by eight pewterers, one of whom was a woman, "une batteresse d'etain." In 1304 the pewterers' guild there was so confirmed in its prosperity that the Master was thenceforth ordered to pay a premium to the State on succeeding to office, unless his father had been master before him. It was doubtless owing to this growing demand for pewter in foreign lands, and, consequently, for the tin which formed so essential an ingredient of it, that in 1305 Edward I. confirmed and enlarged the Charter to the Stanners, relieving them, among other provisions, of all duties; freeing them practically from all responsibility to the general laws except for capital crimes; giving them courts, judges, and a prison of their own; and bestowing upon them the extraordinary privilege of searching for and securing tin and peat wherever they chose in utter disregard of any private ownership in land. The decoration of pewter, to a certain extent, had already begun early in the fourteenth century, though, as has been suggested in the last chapter, it was not apparently as yet undertaken by the pewterers themselves, but by a distinct class of craftsmen, for Jean de Jeandun, writing in 1323, says that there were many chasers of gold, silver, pewter, and bronze on the Grand Pont, and as goldsmiths were not allowed to infringe upon the pewterers' province, nor the pewterers

PLATE XXXVI

1 H. 8" CANDLESTICKS, Scotch. XVIII century.

2 H. 3" D. 5¾" CANDLESTICK, Scotch. XIX century. No marks.

3 H. 7¼" CANDLESTICKS, Dutch. XVIII century.

PLATE XXXVII

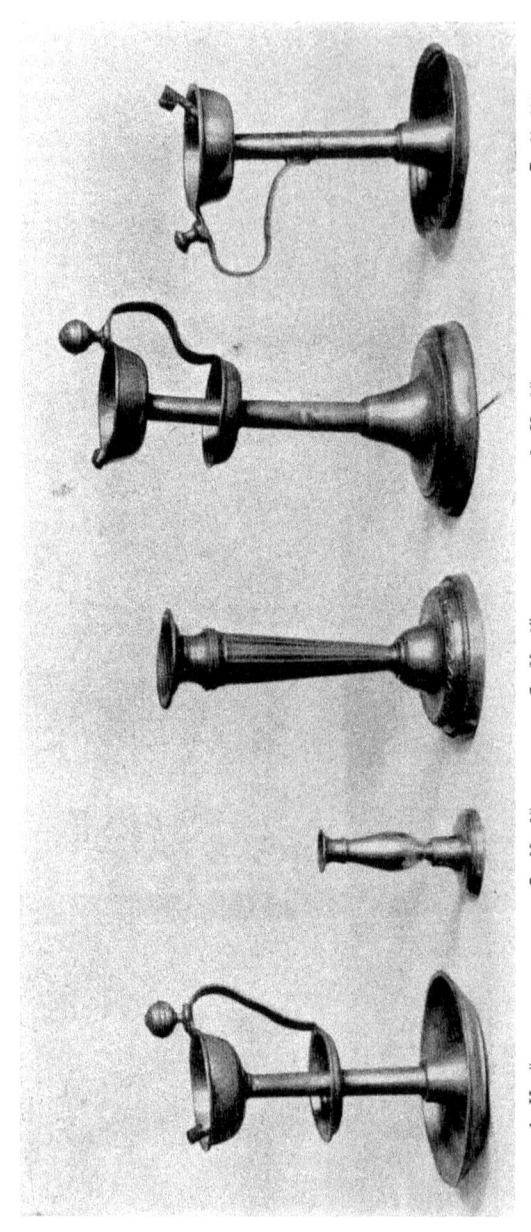

1 H. 9" 2 H. 3¾" 3 H. 7¼" 4 H 9½" 5 H. 8¼"
OIL LAMP, German. TAPER HOLDER, CANDLESTICK, OIL LAMPS, German.
XVIII century. Flemish. French. XVIII century.

BEFORE FIFTEENTH CENTURY

on theirs, it follows that these impartial ornamenters must have been considered independent of both.

Germany by this time had developed a sufficiently important pewter industry of her own to necessitate the formulating of regulations at Augsburg, in 1324, for the visitation of the workshops and investigation of the material used by properly qualified officials, armed with the corresponding powers to punish offenders, and in the same year the name of a pewterer, Carel, is recorded at Nuremberg. Belgium was also well to the for, for at Ath, in 1328, the pewterers' guild was accorded the first place in the civic processions, while a list of pewter belonging to Clement of Hungary, made in the same year, which included one hundred and forty-two porringers and a portable bénitier, or holy-water-holder (*see* Plates V. and VI.), shows that a recognition of the usefulness of pewter was already widely spread in Europe.

In 1333 the town authorities of Poitiers found it advisable to pass an edict against the use of inferior alloys; and the establishment of the craft in London is, for the first time, definitely proved by the record in 1347 of the will of one Nicholas le Peautrer, which is noted in the calendar drawn up for the corporation of the City of London by Dr. Sharpe. The evidence is not, however, of high importance, since the next year witnessed the grant by the Mayor and corporation, in response to the petition of the London pewterers, of those ordinances regulating the conduct of the trade and appointing a Master and Wardens to enforce them, the chief effects of which upon the craft have been already referred to in the last chapter. An interesting sidelight is furthermore thrown by them upon the extent of the manufacture, pots, salers, or salt-cellars, porringers, platters, saucers, dishes, chargers, square pitchers, square cruets, chrismatories, round pots, round cruets, and candlesticks being among the articles specified, after which array the six quart pots purchased by John of France in 1351 present but a humble appearance.

Mons, in Belgium, appears among the centres of pewter making in 1353, and the craft was so well supported at Ghent three years later, that its members supplied no less than thirteen sergeants to the town militia. The pewterers' guild at Rouen emerges from

PLATE XXXXVIII

1 H. 18"   2 H. 15"   3 H. 15"   4 H. 13"   5 H. 14¼"

LAMP TIME-KEEPERS. XVII century.

PLATE XXXIX

1 H. 8½″ D. at base 4¼″   2 H. 9″ D. at base 5¼″   3 H. 8″ D. at base 4″
CANDLESTICKS.

PLATE XL

1 H. 6⅝″   2 8¾″ × 7″   4 H. 6⅝″
CANDLESTICK.   TRAY. XVIII century.   CANDLESTICK.
XVIII century.   XVIII century.

3 H. 4″
INKSTAND.

BEFORE FIFTEENTH CENTURY

its previous obscurity in 1369, when the exchange value of old and new metal was fixed by Royal Letters. An inventory made in 1370 informs us that Henri de Poitiers, Bishop of Troyes, was the owner of fourteen dozen pewter porringers, besides flagons, pots, decanters, and cimaises. These last were vessels chiefly used to contain the ceremonial wine offered to royal personages on their arrival in the neighbourhood of a city wherein they proposed to sojourn for awhile. When the contents had been duly disposed of the Court attendants looked upon the vessels in which they were served as a rightful perquisite, and the thrifty burgers, in consequence, who were put in any case to quite sufficient expense by the honour of the royal visit, economically made them of pewter.

In 1376 the pewterers of Bruges were represented in the town militia by eight sergeants, falling somewhat below the contingent supplied by their brethren of Ghent.

During the closing years of this century mentions of pewter in inventories, wills, and accounts become much more frequent. Thus, in 1380, Michelet the Breton, a pewterer of Paris, supplied six dozen dishes and twelve dozen porringers, weighing in all 474½ marks, to Charles VI., and in the same year a portable bénitier is recorded among the possessions of Jean de Halomesnil, one of the canons of Sainte-Chapelle. Two years later we find the first record of pewter candelabra and chandeliers at Soignies. A reason for the extreme rarity nowadays of this early pewter appears in 1383, when the before-mentioned Michelet the Breton was paid 24 sols 9 deniers of Paris for recasting twenty-four large pewter dishes, and the sum paid also serves to show how slightly the mere workmanship of such things was rewarded, since the same dishes originally cost 119 marks. The labour expended in remaking them must have been exactly the same as was exercised in the first instance, and it therefore follows that three deniers' worth of work went to each mark's weight of metal. A canon of Troyes is found in 1386 as the owner of a good store of pewter, though he is, properly enough, less well provided than his bishop, boasting of only five dozen porringers, with salvers, mugs, and cups; and in the same year the city of Amiens purchased from Thibaut la Rue, "17 poz demi-los," and the city of Rouen a

BEFORE FIFTEENTH CENTURY

gallon flagon which weighed twenty-eight pounds, a moderately cumbersome prize for the official who claimed it even after the "wine of honour" had been finished.

The primitive simplicity was by then beginning to give place to a more pretentious style, and in 1389 the Archbishop of Rheims bequeathed in his will, with eighteen dishes great and small, forty-eight porringers, a square measure, two square quart pitchers, and other vessels, two round pitchers and two measures of three chopins each, all "fasson d'argent," while about the same time one Sebaldus Ruprecht in Germany obtained what must be regarded as an equivocal fame for making and fashioning pewter which could be mistaken for silver.

A woman pewterer, one Isabel de Moncel, is first mentioned by name in 1395 as working at Paris, while in the same city a use of pewter not contemplated by the maker comes to light in 1396, when Jean Lebœuf was accused of striking a fellow toper with a wine measure, thus forestalling by more than four centuries the unnamed individual who knocked the late Mr. Bardell "on the head with a quart pot in a public-house cellar" and caused him, in the eloquent language of Serjeant Buzfuz, to " glide almost imperceptibly from the world, to seek elsewhere for that repose and peace which a custom-house can never afford."

During the fourteenth century, then, we find that the use of pewter was almost entirely confined to the Court, the nobility and higher Church dignitaries, who would seem, however, to have been sufficiently profitable customers, for the English pewterers throughout the last thirty years of it were ceaselessly crying out against the injury inflicted on them by the tinkers and pedlars, who found it worth their while to go about from house to house and town to town in the country recasting damaged pewter. They founded their demand for redress on the plea that these unlicensed workmen adulterated the pewter with so much lead that the vessel afterwards was "not worth the fourth part sold for," and thereby not only defrauded the owner but brought the craft into disrepute. This we may well believe was perfectly true, but it is impossible to avoid suspecting at the same time that the loss of business to themselves arising from this illegal competition was the chief basis of their objection.

PLATE XLI

1 H. 5⅞″
CUP. Scotch.
XVIII century.

2 H. 9¼″
LOVING CUP.
XVIII century.

3   H. 5¼″   4
WINE-CUPS. XVIII century. No marks.

THE FIFTH CHAPTER

SOME FACTS ABOUT PEWTER IN THE FIFTEENTH CENTURY

URING this century the pewterers continued to enjoy exalted patronage. In 1401 Isabella of Bavaria ordered from Jehan de Montrousti nine dozen dishes and twenty-three dozen porringers for her own kitchen and thirty dozen more for the Hôtel St. Pol. An inventory made in the course of the next year at Rouen, quoted by Bapst, as far as its exact meaning is recognisable under the originality of the spelling, serves to show that the tools used by the pewterer in those days were much the same as now, including the lathe with its necessary appurtenances, burnishers, scrapers, a file, various moulds, punches, scales, &c.

Though the manufacture of pewter was by then almost universal in Northern Europe, it is not until 1406 that we discern any evidences of its existence in Spain, but in that year the customary regulations and statutes were drawn up at Barcelona. In 1407 one

OLD PEWTER

Guillebert of Metz is noted as a maker of remarkable works of art in pewter, but no known examples of his handicraft remain. York would seem to have captured at an early date the command of the trade in the north of England, and in 1419 the regulations of her pewterers were codified. These were on the whole much the same as those in force in London, though they appear to have aimed at an even more rigorous exclusiveness, since it was ordained that no one was to set up as a master in the city who had not served his apprenticeship within its walls.

Yet another royal order is recorded for 1422, when Charles VII. of France purchased sixty-four dishes and one hundred and fifty-eight porringers from Jehan Goupil of Tours, but the use of the material had already, in England at least, descended far down in the social scale, for Robert Chichely, Lord Mayor of London, in 1423 ordained, with a quaint preciseness as to detail, "that retailers of ale should sell the same in their houses in pots of pewter sealed and opened, and that whoever carried ale to the buyer should hold the pot in one hand and a cup in the other ; and that all who had pots unsealed should be

PLATE XLII

1 H. 20¼"   2 H. 16"   3 H. 18"
GERMAN GUILD CUPS.

PLATE XLIII

1 H. 10¼"   2 H. 6¼"   3 H. 11⅝"
For Descriptions, see back of Plate.

DESCRIPTIONS OF OBJECTS ON PLATE XLII.

1. Cup, on lid 1721, three shields, right and left a tankard, above I.W.L., below 1713, centre one a church with spire.
2. Flagon, on front IMS 1706, Nuremberg rose on bottom inside, on the handle a shield, IMK, a wall and two turrets
3. Cup, inscribed Johannes George Reichel Johannes Battzer Rellurg, Anno 1693, Christope Stutz.

DESCRIPTIONS OF OBJECTS ON PLATE XLIII.

1. Flagon, German. XVII century.
2. Beaker, Scotch. XVII century.
3. Flagon, German. XVIII century.

THE FIFTEENTH CENTURY

fined." No pronouncement, unluckily, is made as to what material the cup should be made of, so it must remain doubtful whether we have here the earliest example of beer served "in its native pewter," to quote Mr. Robert Sawyer. There is almost as much uncertainty as to the exact meaning of "sealed" in this connection as there has been in magisterial minds of late years anent its exact significance in the Act relating to the sale of intoxicating liquors to infants. Mr. Massé assumes that it means stamped by the maker as a guarantee of the quality of the pewter, but it would seem more probable that the seal was to certify that the vessel held good measure, a point which certainly would more directly concern the customer, as well as the innkeeper, than the nature of the alloy. The spread of pewter among the less exalted is further illustrated in 1427 by the will of John Ely, vicar of Ripon, who left half a garnish and two chargers. The regulations as to the lawful weights of various articles made in 1430 have already been referred to, as have the two forms of the alloy authorised by the Montpelier pewterers in 1437.

The London pewterers were evidently

waxing proud in their growing prosperity by this time, for in 1438 they presumed to add to their ordinances without consulting the Lord Mayor, who promptly asserted his authority and showed his resentment by annulling the additions until he had been petitioned with due humility to allow them. How great this prosperity was is shown by the fact that in 1444 the Warden of the Company thought it advisable to ensure a sufficient supply of that essential ingredient, tin, by obtaining the right to pre-empt one-quarter of all that came into the city. An inventory of the same year shows that John Danby of Alveston, a mere commoner, possessed " ix. pece led and pewd vessell," worth two shillings and fourpence, while in 1453 Jacques Cœur laid in a supply of pewter for his workpeople. As is so often the case with fashions, however, when the common people began to enjoy it the upper classes thought it time to eschew it, and in the inventory of Sir John Fastolfe's possessions in 1459 among nineteen thousand ounces of plate not a grain of pewter is to be found. Yet the noble and royal visitors to subject cities had still to be content with supping their vin d'honneur from humble pewter, at

PLATE XLIV

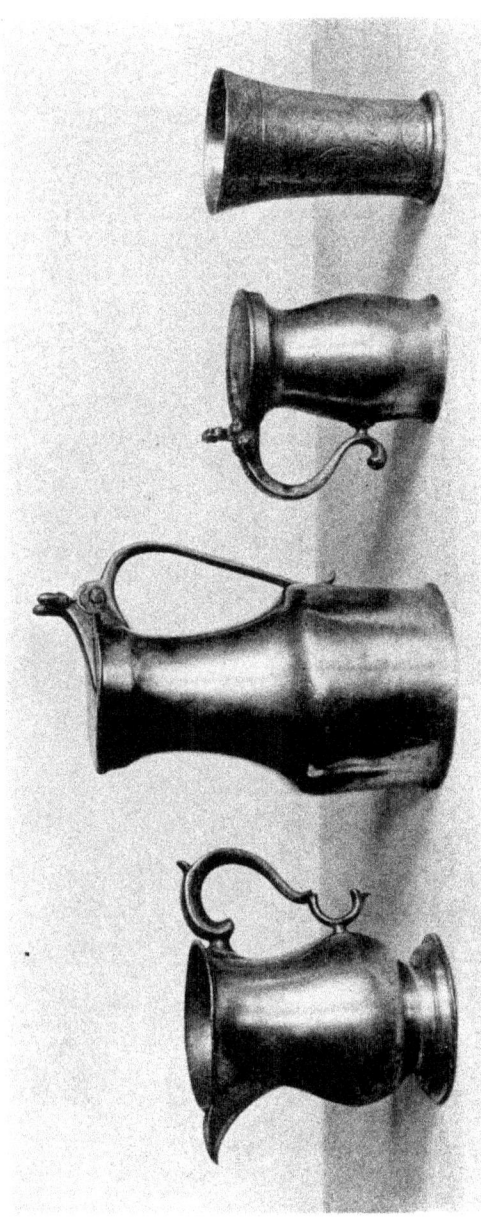

1 H. 7″   TANKARD. Scotch. XVIII century. Marked "Galbraith Glasgow."

2 H. 11″   MEASURE. English. Early XVIII century.

3 H. 6″   MEASURE. English. Early XVIII century.

4 H. 6″   BEAKER. Engraved. Early XVIII century. Mark, a crowned rose.

PLATE XLV

1 D. 13½"   DISH, English. XVII century.
2 H. 7⅞"   TANKARD, German XVIII century.
3 D. 12'   DEEP DISH, Scotch. XVI century.

THE FIFTEENTH CENTURY

any rate at Amiens, where cups for the purpose were again purchased in 1463. The partially religious nature of the London guild is revealed by the mention of a gift made in 1465, in which it is described as "the brotherhood of Our Lady of the Assumption of the pewterer's craft," and the continued use of their products for church purposes by a record made in 1467 of the existence at "St. Stephne's in Colman Streete," of "3 pair of cruets, 22 dishes for the sepulcur, 2 for the pascal, and one on a stokke before Synt John in the church." In the same year the craftsmen of Mons began to mark their wares with a crowned hammer and the word "fin," unless it were spun, in which case a castle and the town arms were used, while pewter imported from England, a common practice abroad at the time, was stamped with a crowned rose. We find in 1470 that even the rival Goldsmiths' Company was investing in pewter, one pound seventeen shillings and sixpence being paid that year "for a garnish of 2 dozen pewter vessels to serve the company," in spite of the fact that the pewterers were then imitating the designs of the goldsmiths, and

OLD PEWTER

in France were buying from them drawings, and patterns in pewter and clay. About the same time Buschius of Hildesheim undertook a progress for the purpose of investigating the state of the Saxon convents, and in his account pewter bulks largely. The convent at St. Cyr owned two hundred amphoræ, flagons and tankards, which does not point to any excessive austerity; that of the Holy Cross of Erfurth one hundred and fifty amphoræ, seventy cups, twelve jugs, and thirty-three porringers; the Cistercians of St. Martin had also one hundred and fifty amphoræ, flagons and porringers; but the White Ladies of Erfurth, either owing to poverty or a stricter rule, were satisfied with only forty-one amphoræ, porringers, and four flagons. The year 1473 was a notable one for pewterers in England, for in the course of it King Edward IV. testified his royal approval of their labours by conferring on their Company a formal Charter confirming the privileges they enjoyed and the powers they had presumably exercised so satisfactorily, and in 1478 the Duke of Burgundy followed suit by establishing guilds in many of the cities in his dominions. A clear idea of the immense

THE FIFTEENTH CENTURY

proportions the trade had assumed may be gathered from the fact that in 1481 one record of the metal employed for organ pipes alone, a blend of six parts of tin with four of lead, accounts for fourteen thousand five hundred pounds. "A hoole garnish of peautre vessel, two round basin of peautre" are found in the will of Elizabeth Lady Uvedale in 1487, and pewter bottles in the "Livre des Mestiers" of Charles V., while from an inventory of the goods of the Pewterers' Guild of London made two years later we learn that their common seal bore "the ymage of thassumpčon of our blessyd lady gravyn theryn of silver." The fact that the Company guaranteed by a stamp the quality of pewter is confirmed by the entry in 1492 of the purchase of four new "marking irons for Holoweware men."

Scotland, according to Mr. Ingleby Wood, lagged far behind her southern sister in the pewterer's craft, and this he suggests was due in part to the greater general poverty, in part to the absence of native tin, which must have added very seriously to the original cost of the raw material, and in part to the facility with which the ware could be smuggled into

OLD PEWTER

the country, in defiance of all statutes, from the Dutch, Flemish, and French ports, with which so large a general trade was carried on. Be the causes what they may, it is not until the very end of the century, in 1496, that we get the first actual record of pewter-making in Scotland, when a second "Seal of Cause" or Charter of Incorporation was granted by the Provost, Magistrates, and Town Council of Edinburgh to the Hammermen of the City, in whose ranks, for the first time, the peudrars, together with the coppersmiths, appear, the first Seal of Cause issued in 1483 naming only blacksmiths, goldsmiths, saddlers, cutlers, and armourers. We learn from this how greatly the arrangements in Scotland differed from those in England, where each of these crafts had a distinct guild of its own. In Scotland, on the contrary, all the tradesmen whose work was in the main executed with a hammer, except the carpenters, masons, and usually plumbers, were enrolled in one comprehensive Corporation, which, though differing in its exact composition at various times and in different places, generally extended to glovers, lorimers, buckle-makers, sword-cutlers, gunsmiths, potters and braziers at

1 H. 9¾" 2 H. 10¼" 3 H. 9¼" 4 H. 9¼"
TANKARDS, German. XVII century.

PLATE XLVII

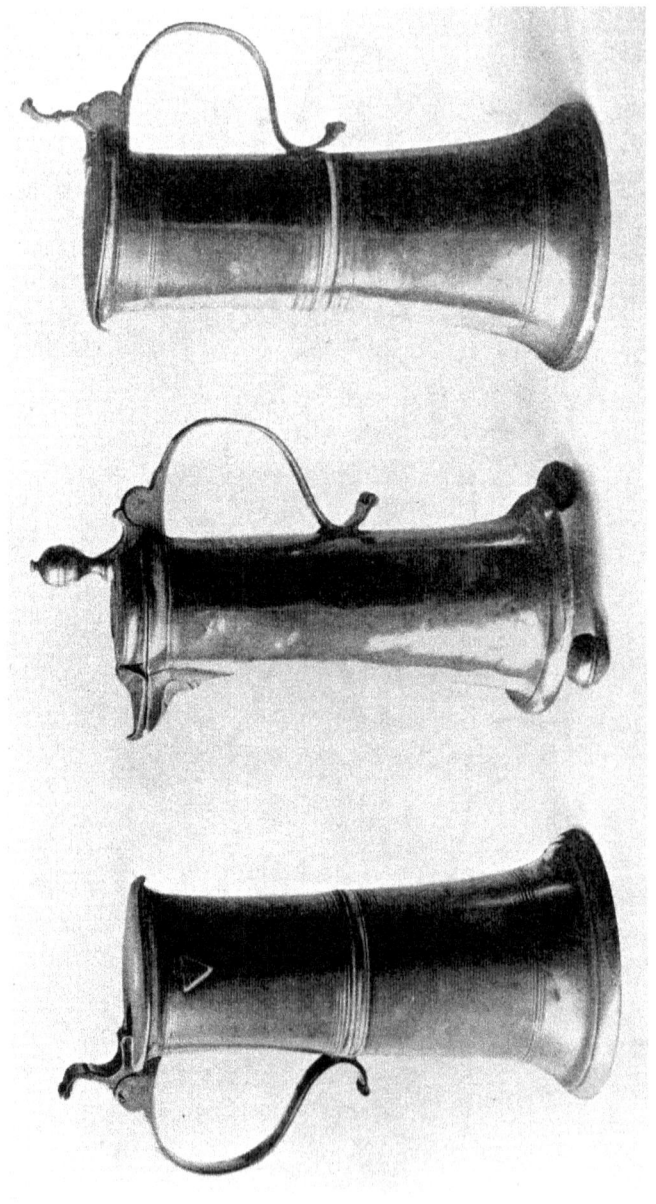

1 H. 11⅞"   2 H. 12⅝"   3 H. 12½"

GERMAN TANKARDS, XVII and XVIII century.

THE FIFTEENTH CENTURY

Perth, and sword-guard makers at Dundee; skinners, glaziers, wrights and potters at Aberdeen; clock-makers, bell-makers and plumbers at Glasgow; and later on white-ironsmiths, or tinsmiths as we should say nowadays, watch-makers, carriage-makers, bell-hangers, and at St. Andrews even such alien trades as dyers, painters, and stationers.

The main features of the development of pewter-ware during the fifteenth century were the increasing range downwards in the social scale of its domestic use, the consequent growth in numbers of the craftsmen working in it—Bapst has collected the names of one hundred and sixteen workers during that century in France alone—and the beginning of the custom among the wealthier classes of having their pewter so lavishly adorned that the cost became prohibitive to the lower orders, thus ensuring to themselves for a while longer freedom from the competition of the vulgar.

THE SIXTH CHAPTER
SOME FACTS ABOUT PEWTER IN THE SIXTEENTH CENTURY

IN England at the beginning of the sixteenth century, pewter, according to the Northumberland household book, was still considered too expensive to be common, but the trade had nevertheless grown to be so important, and the temptations to fraudulent practices on the part of its followers so strong and apparently so frequently yielded to, that in 1503 an Act of Parliament (19 Henry VII. c. 6) was passed to compel every maker to mark his ware with a recognisable touch of his own, to forbid him to sell outside his own business premises except in open fair and market, and to put down the use of false weights and scales. The legal mind about the same time seems to have realised that the increasing independence of the great City companies, if not dangerous to the Crown, was decidedly inimical to its own financial interests, and that certain customary regulations adopted

PLATE XLVIII

1 H. 9¾″
PEG TANKARD, Danish. With engraved decoration inscribed Kleinreide (Klein Rheide, Schleswig), 1783. Mark, a heart transfixed with arrows with initials and date, LHT 1781.

2 H. 10¼″
JUG, English. XVIII century.

3 H. 7¾″
TANKARD, Swedish 1844. Marks, Arms of Sweden, 04·IBL, and shield of arms.

THE SIXTEENTH CENTURY

by them had the evil effect of preventing many fat pickings from reaching the coffers of the law. The remedy was attempted in 1504 by an Act providing that no ordinance adopted by any one of them should be valid and binding until it had obtained the formal approval of the Chancellor or some other court official, which doubtless meant fees, and at the same time abrogating the rule which forbade brother-members of a guild from going to law with one another in the courts, but compelled them to bring all disputes for arbitration by the wardens and councils, which certainly meant fees.

The "silver fashion" continued to wax in favour with the wealthy and the merely useful to decline, if we may judge by the fact that in 1507 the Duke of Burgundy owned three pitchers and three ewers of a decorative character, and only thirty-two plates, the same number of porringers and a mustard for practical purposes. At the same time the Duke of Bourbonnays had three quart flagons, three pitchers, and three ewers, and in the following year the city of Amiens ordered from Pierre Hemeron four small ewers of fine pewter "fasson d'argent." The English

Parliament again took cognisance of the craft in 1512, in response to a complaint that "evil-disposed persons" went about the country buying pewter and brass, which was generally stolen, and afterwards sold it clandestinely to "strangers" who carried it overseas; that the same persons were in the habit of recasting old vessels, adulterating the material in the process, and, furthermore, used beams and scales so "deceivable and false" "that one of them will stand even with 12 lb. weight at the one end against a quarter of a lb. at the other," which certainly seems carrying fraud to excess; and the penalty of losing the beam and paying a fine of twenty shillings, or, in default, of remaining in the stocks until the next market and elevated on the pillory as long as that lasted, does not sound unduly severe in comparison with the fine of ten pounds incurred by selling pewter otherwise than previously ordained. The hospitality of Amiens would seem to have been inexhaustible, for in 1516 it is again found buying thirty-five small pewter mugs from Jeanne d'Avesne for the purpose of presenting the wine of loyal greeting to François I. and Louise of Savoy. 1518 brings the first inti-

PLATE L

    1   2   3 H. 5½″   4   5
CREAM-JUG   MEASURE   CREAM-JUG
      SALT-CELLAR   EGG-CUP
English. XVIII century.

PLATE LI

 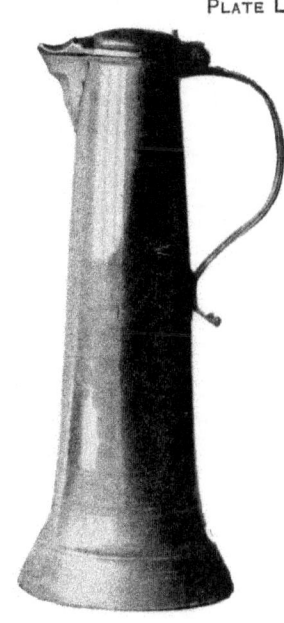

H. 11½″
A PAIR OF TANKARDS, German. XVIII century.

THE SIXTEENTH CENTURY

mation of the Incorporation of Hammermen at Perth, but there is good reason for believing that the book of records bearing this date had predecessors long since destroyed, and in the same year the town authorities of Edinburgh drew up regulations concerning the stamping of the vessels used by taverners, in order to ensure their containing good measure, a plug or "talpoun" on the inside of the neck indicating the height to which each was to be filled. In 1535 we first hear of the Hammermen of the burgh of the Cannongate, who had an Incorporation of their own distinct from that of Edinburgh, and that year appealed for leave to build an altar in the abbey church and dedicate it to St. Eloy, always in Scotland the patron saint of hammermen. On the face of it the offer would seem all to the good of the church, yet for some reason it was not accepted by the abbot until eleven years later.

The English makers about this time began apparently to be troubled by foreign competition. Whether any of the ware of Martin Harscher, a German pewterer who died in 1523 at the age of eighty-three, which was proudly asserted to be superior in quality to English pewter, found its way over here is doubtful, but it was considered desirable, in days when Members of Parliament had no Free Trade bogey to fright them, by an Act passed in 1538, to forbid all importation of foreign pewter, to deny to foreigners the right of working in England, and even to endeavour to prevent Englishmen from working abroad.

The Incorporation of Hammermen at Glasgow is first mentioned in 1536, but pewterers are not particularly specified, probably, as Mr. Wood suggests, because they were too few to make it worth while, being merely included in the comprehensive "others within the burgh." The dissolution of the monasteries in 1537, or, rather, the inventories of their contents which that high-handed proceeding gave rise to, might well have been expected to throw a flood of light upon the variety of domestic utensils in pewter employed at the time; but as a matter of fact, whether the Commissioners did not consider it as worthy of notice, or whether the monks were too wealthy to condescend to such base material, very little of it appears in any of the records, and the chief fact we learn is that what we now

THE SIXTEENTH CENTURY

call porringers were known as "counterfettes or podingers."

The earliest ordinances of the Hammermen of St. Andrews bear date 1539, but in this case also it is supposed that older ones existed but have been lost. In the same year King James V. persuaded a number of foreign craftsmen from Holland, France, and Spain to settle in Scotland, in order, doubtless, that his subjects might learn from them, and it is at least probable that some pewterers were among them; and in the next year the same enlightened monarch conferred upon the Hammermen of the Cannongate a ratification of their "Seal of Cause," which confirmed, and to some degree extended, their privileges.

At the same time in England the pewterers of York were deciding that every pewterer was to stamp his handiwork with his own mark, a "counterpayne" of which was to be kept in the "common chambre" for purposes of identification, in which course they were evidently following in the footsteps of their brethren in London, who already, according to an inventory of the date, had "a table of pewter, with every man's mark therein," which has unfortunately long since disappeared.

OLD PEWTER

The various corporations obviously found it easier to lay down rules and regulations than to enforce them, for again and again we find one or another re-affirming laws which were supposed to have been long in force. Thus, in 1543, the Hammermen of St. Andrews found it necessary to repeat an Act governing the admission of none but those whose competence in their particular craft had been thoroughly established, not only to the satisfaction of the selected officers belonging to it, but of the Provost and Magistrates of the city, and in the course of the same year the Edinburgh authorities were obliged to renew and amplify their Act relating to taverners' measures. Two years later the Edinburgh Trade Incorporations became owners of the Chapel and Hospital of St. Mary Magdalen, and the Charter of Dedication was drawn up in accordance with the wishes of one Janet Rhynd, to whose generous gift of two thousand pounds Scots, or one hundred and sixty-six pounds sterling, the completion of the building was due.

Meantime in France the manufacture of what would nowadays be called "art" pewter was progressing so rapidly that the gold and

PLATE LII

1 H. 13⅝"   2 H. 12⅛"

3 H. 21¾"

GERMAN GUILD TANKARDS

THE SIXTEENTH CENTURY

silversmiths of Paris began to take fright at the encroachments of their rivals upon their especial domains which had clearly been initiated; and in 1545 they appealed for an enactment forbidding the pewterers to work in any other metal, while they on their part, in order to balance things and forestall a grievance on their rivals' side, undertook never to work in pewter.

The first glimpse of pewterers in Perth is gained by an odd side-light in 1546, when the hammermen forbade the apprentices, among them the "pewteraris," to play football on the historical Inch, whereon Hal of the Wynd fought his famous fight. 1550 is famous in the annals of purely decorative pewter as the probable birth-year of François Briot, in whose hands it reached its highest culmination. Though over-elaborated and ill suited to the material, there is no denying to his masterpieces a wonderful fertility of invention and consummate finish of workmanship. His finest work is undoubtedly the salver with a nude figure of Temperance, seated and holding a cup, in the centre, allegorical representations of the elements surrounding her, and the sciences on the rim, the whole accompanied and embellished by a variety of Renaissance ornamentation. Specimens of this may be found both in the British Museum and at South Kensington.

The beginnings of a revolution which was destined in after years to cause the London pewterers much vexation of spirit, is indicated in 1552 by the rules promulgated compelling the makers of the pewter lids attached to stoneware vessels to bring their whole weekly output every "Satterdaye" to the Hall in order that, if they were judged sufficiently well and truly wrought, the lids might be stamped outside with the mark of the Hall as well as with the maker's own personal mark. Traces of the Reformation which had devastated church and church plate seventeen years before probably linger in the record on the register of Waltham Abbey Church of the purchase, in 1554, of a chrismatory and pix in pewter, the former costing three shillings and sixpence, the latter two shillings. The order against buying by night from unauthorised or suspicious characters, which has been already referred to, was passed in 1555.

The high respect with which pewter was

THE SIXTEENTH CENTURY

regarded in Scotland is shown by an entry in the town records of Edinburgh, dated June 27, 1559. In consequence of threatened disturbances the treasures of the Church of St. Giles were to be removed and distributed for safety amongst various presumably trustworthy members of the congregation, who did not, however, apparently justify in all cases the confidence so rashly reposed in them, since even " Johne Charterhous, elder, Dean of the Guild," in spite of his responsible position, never, as far as we know, could be persuaded to restore the " twa candelstyks of tin " which had been deemed worthy to adorn the " hie altar " until untoward circumstances flung them into his too conscientious custody. Another of many quaint and interesting records which Mr. Wood has unearthed for us is found at Perth next year, where, among the duties prescribed for an apprentice who wished to qualify as master, we discover the obligatory presentation of a football. The same year brought about the downfall of the Roman Catholic Church in Scotland and the establishment of Presbyterianism on its ruins, and in the process, what with the vessels which were carried abroad by the departing faithful, those which came into the care of such guardians as Johne Charterhous, those like the possessions of St. Giles's which were sold in 1561 for the public benefit, and those that fell victims to the zeal of the Reformers, the pre-Reformation church plate without a known exception disappeared.

In 1564 the question of apprentices was finally settled for England on a definite basis. In accordance with a statute passed in the previous year, it was ordained that every freeman of the Company was entitled to take one apprentice, while the Master and Wardens were allowed three, provided that at the same time they employed not less than two journeymen. They did not, it would seem, approve of the decorative debauch in progress among their brethren across the Channel, supporting whole-heartedly the rigour of the game, for while a Nuremberg pewterer, Melchior Koch, who died in 1567, was gaining fame for a process, the secret of which he carried with him to the grave, of making an alloy which closely resembled gold, the Englishmen prohibited absolutely the application of gilding or painting to the surface of vessels with the exception, allowed by an Act of 1564, of small

1 H. 12¾"   2 H. 14¼"   3 H. 13¼"

GERMAN GUILD TANKARDS. XVII to XVIII century.

PLATE LIV

H. 6¼″

MEASURE or TANKARD, German. Late XVII century.

PLATE LV

1 H. 5″   2 H. 6¼″   3 H. 5½″   4 H. 4½″

SCOTCH MEASURES. XVIII century.

PLATE LVI

1 H. 4½″   2 H. 3⅞″   3 H. 3¾″   4 H. 3½″   5 H. 3¼″

MEASURES.

THE SIXTEENTH CENTURY

articles which had been made solely to be given away as presents by the maker, a curious illustration of the minute details with which the makers of the ordinances concerned themselves.

The need of some distinguishing mark to indicate the quality was first officially recognised in Scotland in 1567, when an Act of King James VI. provided that " fyne tyn pewder " was to be marked with a crown and hammer, and the second quality with the maker's name, with the usual penalties of fine and confiscation if the stamps were absent or undecipherable. Before 1570 Dundee had followed Edinburgh in her resolve to ensure for her citizens good measure from the taverners, and " ane iron stamp to mark ye tinn stoopis " was in the charge of the Dean of Guilds there that year.

In England and on the Continent pewterware had by the middle of the century become almost an inevitable part of the plenishing of every respectable family, so that in 1572 a simple draper of Paris could bequeath to his heir " six plates, two eared and two deep and four shallow porringers, three large dishes, three sauce-boats, a mustard, a salt, a couple of basins, a water-pitcher, and a pint pot." The pewterers, in fact, were beginning to boast, especially in Germany, that they could and did make everything in their material that the gold or silversmith could produce, though they did not at that time confine themselves strictly to pewter, for the pewterer in a "Treatise on Industries," by Harman Schoper, written in 1573, is made to declare: " I make vases of all sorts of molten metals." It was, therefore, scarcely to be wondered at that in 1579 some candlesticks made in pewter by Peter Schmitt having attracted too much approval, the goldsmiths of Nuremberg secured the adoption of a self-denying ordinance, similar to the earlier one agreed to in Paris, consenting to forego the right of themselves working in pewter, on condition that the pewterers did not intrude upon their speciality.

The first " Seal of Cause " was granted to the Hammermen of Aberdeen in 1579, but from references in the document it is clear that they must have existed as a properly organised body before the Reformation of 1560, since it is remarked that they still owned and worshipped at an altar to St. Eloi,

THE SIXTEENTH CENTURY

and, strangely enough, still lighted it with candles made, as was very general in Scotland, from wax procured in the form of fines from offenders against their ordinances. For many years, wherever incorporations of the various crafts existed in Scotland there had been constant friction between the deacons and other officers elected by the members and the town magistrates, who represented for the most part the wealthier merchants, and, jealous doubtless of the increasing power and unity of the craftsmen, endeavoured to interfere more closely and frequently in their affairs than the victims deemed desirable, while the magistrates on their part were constantly complaining that the deacons were always striving to exceed their lawful powers. The question was grappled with, and in the end set at rest by an Act of James VI., passed in 1581, which by granting a Charter to the crafts raised them to the same level as the merchants, and though these last can scarcely have been well pleased at their practical defeat, peace seems to have reigned thereafter. Dating from 1587 the first record book existing of the Dundee Incorporation was, as usual, evidently not the earliest, but the history of this body is not of great importance to us, since one Master Gray is the only "pewderer" belonging to it.

The same year in England saw the publication of Harrison's "Description of England in Shakespeare's Time," which gives many interesting pictures of the life of the period, not omitting references to pewter, which he notes is becoming more frequent. " For so common were all sorts of treene stuffe in olde time, that a man should hardly find four pieces of pewter (of which one was peradventure a salt) in a good farmer's house. But now a farmer will think his gains very small if towards the end of his term he cannot have a fair garnish of pewter on his cupboard, a bowl for wine (if not a whole neast), and a dozen of spoons to furnish up the suit." As for the upper classes, he says: "Likewise in the houses of knights, gentlemen, merchantmen, and some other wealthy citizens, it is not geson (unusual) to behold generallie their great provision of tapestrie, Turkie work, pewter, brass, and fine linen, and thereto costlie cupboards of plate with five or six hundred or a thousand pounds to be deemed by estimation," a passage which strikingly recalls Shakes-

PLATE LVII

1 D. 5½″
WINE-TASTER, English. XVII century. Dug up in Tottenham Court Road.

2 H. 11″
WINE-MEASURE, German. XVIII century.

3 H. 9″
WINE-MEASURE, German. XVIII century.

PLATE LVIII

1 D. 11″
TWO-HANDLED BOWL.

2 H. 6″ D. 4″
WATER-JUG. English. XVIII century.

3 H. 4″ D. 3″
RICE BOILER. French. XVIII century.

4 D. of
PLATE, one of a set of six. English. XVIII century. Stamped with initials ICB and IBB

5 H. 7½
MEASURE. English. XVIII century.

THE SIXTEENTH CENTURY

peare's own description of a well-provided house which he put into the mouth of Gremio, in the *Taming of the Shrew*, act ii., scene 1.

> "First, as you know, my house within the city
> Is richly furnished with plate and gold;
> Basins and ewers to lave her dainty hands;
> My hangings all of Tyrian tapestry;
> In ivory coffers I have stuffed my crowns;
> In cypress chests my arras counterpoints,
> Costly apparel, tents and canopies,
> Fine linen, Turkey cushions boss'd with pearl,
> Valance of Venice gold in needlework,
> Pewter and brass and all things that belong
> To house or housekeeping."

What the pewter probably consisted of is made clear by an inventory made in 1594 of the contents of a house at Gillingham, occupied by Sir William Fairfax, as reproduced in *Archæologia*, vol. xlviii. In the "wineseller one quart pewter pott," in the pantry two basins and ewers of pewter valued at fourteen shillings and four pence, and two pewter trays valued at ten shillings; in the "kytchine" twenty-four saucers, twenty-four dishes great and small, twenty-four platters great and small, four chargers, and twelve more dishes. There were also twelve saucers, twelve "sallite dishes," twenty-four great dishes, eighteen great platters, and "i charger of the greatest sort," which were all new. The value of the whole collection being eighteen pounds, six shillings and eightpence. Perhaps the shortcomings of some of these very saucers may have led the Company in the following year to decide that never more should saucers be wrongfully finished by turning on a lathe, but duly and properly hammered " uppon payne of forfayture."

That the French merchants did not fall behind the standard of luxury attained by their English neighbours is shown by the inventory of one Pierre de Capdeville of Bordeaux in 1591, which, in spite of some uncertainty as to the exact meaning of some of the distinctive descriptions, gives a good idea of the state of bourgeois comfort at the time. In addition to a variety of jugs and measures used in the business of selling wine, he possessed a ewer, two flagons, two ollieres, which may have been cruets or oil-jars, six great dishes "du grande molle," thirteen dishes "du deuxième molle," one "du tiers molle," eight "du petit molle" (the terms referring perhaps to the size of the moulds in which they were cast), thirty-six round plates,

PLATE LIX

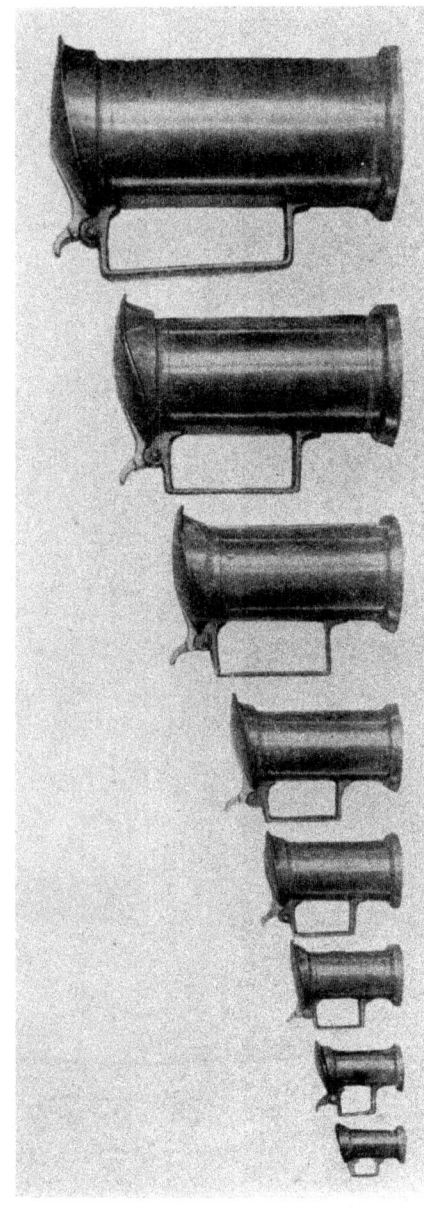

SET OF FRENCH MEASURES. XVIII century.   Ranging from 2" to 10" high.

Plate LX

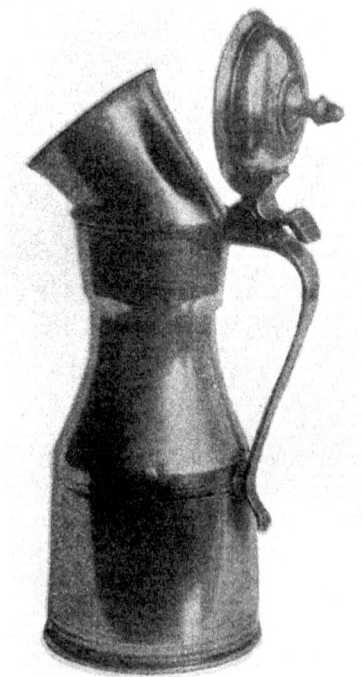

H. 11¾"
TAPPIT HEN. XVIII century.

THE SIXTEENTH CENTURY

fourteen-eared porringers, seven sauce-boats, two large "gardelles," and one hundred pounds weight of old pewter, while he was, furthermore, so far in the fashion as to own a basin and ewer or cistern of ornamental ware.

Imperfect as are the records of the Incorporations of Hammermen in most Scottish cities, those of Stirling are more than usually so, only two which in any way concern us, covering the period from 1596 to 1620, remaining; and though, like all these ordinances, they contain much unconscious humour, and throw considerable light on the life of the time, they do not to any appreciable extent advance our knowledge of the state of the pewterer's craft in the burgh. The most notable fact revealed by them is that between 1599 and 1620 there were four men practising the trade there, a surprising number considering the size of the place, surpassing, as Mr. Wood points out, Aberdeen, Dundee, then the second town in Scotland, St. Andrews and Perth, in the minute-book of whose Incorporation the first name of a freeman "peutherer" does not appear till 1597.

The confirmation by letters patent of the

London Company's privilege of charging a royalty on the smelting and casting of tin, obtained in 1598, brings the history of pewter in the sixteenth century to a close. The most remarkable point in it is the still further widening of the social field in which it came into common use in England, though this was perhaps not altogether without certain incidental disadvantages from the pewterer's point of view. Whether it were cause and effect due to a resentment on the part of fashion against this increasing employment of pewter by the commonalty, or mere coincidence arising out of the growing prosperity inaugurated by the reign of peace which ensued from the overthrow of Richard on Bosworth Field and the accession to the throne of Henry VII., it would be hard to say; but, in England at any rate, even in the opening years of the century, we begin to discover evidences of a steady tendency among the higher classes towards the uses of the more precious metals. In 1501 the banquet given in honour of the politic marriage of Arthur Tudor, the king's ill-fated eldest son and heir, to the scarcely less unfortunate Catherine of Arragon, is stated

PLATE LXI

TAPPIT HENS, the large ones are Imperial quarts, 10⅝" high.

PLATE LXII

H. 12½"

JUG, English. XVII century.

THE SIXTEENTH CENTURY

to have been served on gold plate enriched with pearls and other gems at a total cost of more than twenty thousand pounds; while the accounts given some years later by Robert Amadel and Cavendish of the plate belonging to Cardinal Wolsey read more like pages from the "Arabian Nights" than sober statements of fact. Setting aside such objects as an image of the Virgin and great candlesticks, for which pewter would have been inappropriate, we find three chargers weighing nine hundred and sixty-eight ounces, twenty-two dishes weighing four hundred and fifty-one ounces, and so on. So prodigious was the amount, that even at great banquets a large proportion of it was reserved solely for display. "There was," says Cavendish, speaking of such occasions, "a cupboard as long as the chamber was in breadth, with six deskes in height, garnished with guilt plate, and the nethermost deske was garnyshed all with gold plate, having with lights one pair of candlesticks with silver and guilt, being curiously wrought, which cost three hundred marks. This cupboard was barred round about that no man might come nigh it, for there was none of all this plate touched—there was

OLD PEWTER

sufficient besides." As this example was certainly followed, though less lavishly perhaps by smaller men, the great Cardinal was clearly no good friend to the pewterers; and they, at least, can have felt no great reason to lament his fall.

Other noticeable features in this century are the continued growth of the craft in Scotland, the rapid development of the manufacture of highly decorated ware in France and Germany, and the regrettable and wholly irreparable destruction of church plate during the Reformation in England and Scotland.

THE SEVENTH CHAPTER
SOME FACTS ABOUT PEWTER IN THE SEVENTEENTH CENTURY

ROUBLES began to thicken round the London pewterers during this century. As early as 1601 the provincial competition was making itself so markedly felt that they resolved to insist that thenceforth no craftsman under their control should work publicly in an open shop, thereby giving " occasion that pewterers of the country and others shall come to great lyght of farther knowleg to the great hindraunce of the Company," and so serious did they deem the danger to be that a first failure to comply with the requirements of the ordinance was punishable by a fine of thirteen shillings and fourpence, a second by one of twenty shillings, and the third by expulsion, so that " No brother of the Company shall buy and sell with them," an ancient precedent for boycotting.

1602 is notable as the date inscribed on the most interesting surviving specimen of

Scottish pewter, the Pirley-Pig of Dundee, which is one of the very few examples, showing added exterior ornament. It is a flattened sphere six inches in diameter and three in height, with a narrow opening in one side for the insertion of coins, and was used for many years to hold the fines for non-attendance paid by members of the Council. For a time it disappeared, but by a most fortunate chance was rediscovered in 1839 in a heap of old metal ear-marked for the foundry, and now once more forms one of the treasures of the Town Hall.

To the collector 1603 is not without importance, as in that year by a Canon of the Reformed Church of England it was required that the wine should be brought "to the Communion-table in a clean and sweet standing pot or stoup of pewter—if not of purer metal," and it is, therefore, safe to assume that no pewter church flagons are of earlier date. That this permission to use pewter was promptly taken advantage of is shown by an entry at Strood near Rochester in 1607 of " the purchase from Robert Ewer (for 9*s.* 6*d.*) Two pewter pots to serve the wine at the Communion"; while one still existing at

PLATE LXIV

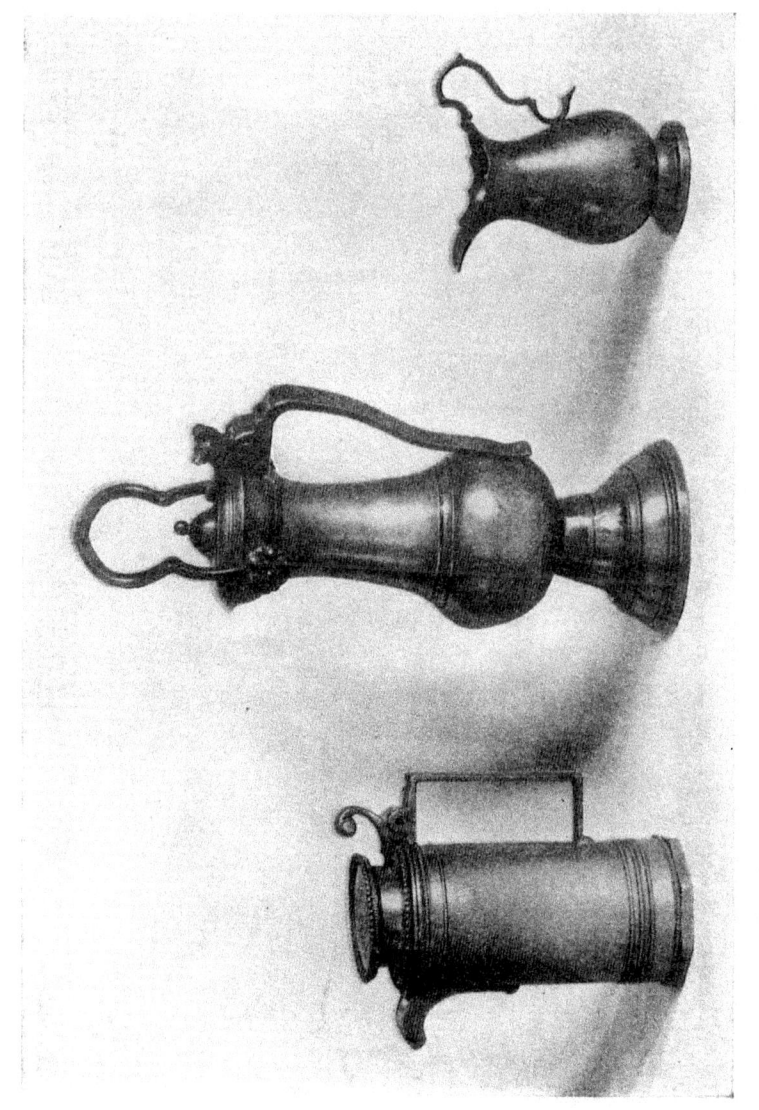

1 H. 6¼″ COVERED JUG. Archangel mark.

2 H. 7¾″ FLAGON.

3 H. 4¾″ CREAM-JUG.

PLATE LXIII

1 H. 11¾"
FLAGON. Probably Scotch.
XVIII century.

2 H. 13"
IMITATION CHINESE
FLAGON. Dutch. XVII
century.

3 H. 13¾"
FLAGON, German.
XVII century.

THE SEVENTEENTH CENTURY

Werrington in Northamptonshire bears an inscription, " Ex dono Edmundi Pennye et Franciscæ uxoris ejus ad usum Capellæ de Werrington 1609."

An example of seemingly calm appropriation of another man's ideas, bearing the date 1611, is to be seen at the Victoria and Albert Museum in the form of a salver of Nuremberg pewter which is practically a reproduction of Briot's Temperantia salver, though it is unblushingly signed SCULPEBAT GASPARD ENDERLEIN, and stamped with his initials G. E.

About this time we begin to perceive an augmenting activity in the craft in England, as indicated by the lengthening catalogue of articles turned out. Among the new names extracted by Mr. Welch from a list made by the Company in 1612 are " chapnets," small vessels for church use, weighing, according to size, one pound and a half or one pound the half dozen ; great beakers, both wrought and plain, middle, small, and children's beakers, large and small beer bowls, large wrought cups, two sizes of French cups, "spowt potts" of various capacities, hawkesbills and ravensbills, which were ewers of different sorts, named perhaps from the beak-like shape of the spout; thurndells and half thurndells, according to Mr. Massé, on the authority of Mr. St. John Hope, a Wiltshire name for vessels containing three pints; and a number of measures, "new quarts, new great, small, and halfe potts, hooped thurndells, Winchester quarts and pints, with or without lidds, long-hooped Winchester pyntes, and Jeayes danske potts," which last are a mystery. The rigorous distinctions between the various branches of craftsmen seem to have been somewhat relaxed about the same period, for the Triflers were including not a little hollow-ware in their output.

The curious independence of the Scottish towns in those days of bad roads and little travel is suggested by the fact that only in 1614 did the Incorporation of Dundee ordain the hall-marking by the Dean of Guild and Town Baillie of tavern measures, nearly a century after Edinburgh had adopted the same sensible course, although as early as 1563, and again in 1568 and 1613, stern punishment had been provided for the use of false measures.

Still new uses for pewter come to light in

THE SEVENTEENTH CENTURY

a list of "trifles" in 1614, such as basins, bowls, pastie plates, pye coffins, limbecks, cefters, and still-heads, so that it is small wonder that in my lord Northampton's kitchens that year the weight of the pewter amounted to three hundred pounds. Thirteen candlesticks of pewter form a noteworthy item in the inventory of Sir Thomas Hoskyns of Oxted, dated 1615; the rest, however, consisting of eight dozen dishes of all sorts, four dozen saucers, and four flagons, is of the usual type of kitchen furniture.

A second wave of revolution swept over the Church of Scotland in 1617, when James I. (VI. of Scotland) forced upon his old kingdom the form of worship prevailing in his new one, under the name of Episcopalianism, and the change of ritual unquestionably contributed to the destruction of much of any plate that had survived from 1567. It also brought into ecclesiastical use, apparently for the first time, a new vessel in the "laver," a form of flagon, usually with a narrow spout, which was used either for pouring the water at baptism on to the face of the child or simply to convey the water to the font. No pewterer is especially mentioned as a member of the

Incorporation of St. Andrews until 1619, and Mr. Wood conjectures that the supplies of ware which must have been demanded by the castle, the university, and the cathedral, were obtained from the gypsies and other wandering unfreeman, who are known to have driven a thriving trade in Scotland just as did the "deceivable hawkers" in England, for whose suppression the London Company were once more clamouring in 1621 as they had done ineffectually so many times before. A further element of tribulation for it appears about this time under the guise of "the Crooked Lane men" whose ware was asserted by it in 1634 to be a "counterfeiting of the reall commodity of Tynn." What this ware was actually made of cannot be stated with absolute certainty. That it was not regarded as fradulent, except by the pewterers, who can scarcely be considered as independent or disinterested judges, is clear, since their hostile attempts were unsuccessful; and, as workers in tin-plate, under the name of white-ironsmiths, were accepted as journeymen by the Corporation of Aberdeen as early as 1649, and as full freemen of that of Glasgow in 1652, it is scarcely a rash conclusion

PLATE LXV

1 D. 8" BOWL. 2 D. 22½" DISH, English. Dated 1689. 3 D. 6¾" PLATE one of six English. XVIII century. 4 D. 8" BOWL.

PLATE LXVI

1 H. 8"
JUG, French. XVIII century.

2 H. 8¼" D. 7¾"
JUG, English. XVIII century.

3 H. 7"
BEER-JUG, English. XVIII century.

THE SEVENTEENTH CENTURY

that in these obnoxious Crooked Lane men we have the first of those tinsmiths whose handiwork in years to come was fated to play no small part in the overthrow of the pewterer's craft.

It is rather sad in the face of this aggressive eagerness on the side of the pewterers to protect " his Maties subjects" from "deceipt or wrong" to find that they were themselves engaged at the very time in marking their wares in a manner so closely resembling the four hall-marks which the Goldsmiths' Company stamped on real plate, that in 1635 the latter appealed for redress to the Privy Council, and that in response the Court of Aldermen ordained that the pewterer should use only one stamp, though he might add the arms or sign of the purchaser on his desiring it.

Once more, in 1638, there came an upheaval in the Church of Scotland, when the people, who had always more or less hated and actively resented it, revolted against Episcopalianism, and pledged themselves to the New Covenant, but the result of this was probably, at any rate at first, an increase in the use of pewter for church vessels, the more precious metals being absorbed in providing means for carrying on the conflict which followed. 1640 is the earliest date on the first of the touch-plates still preserved at Pewterers' Hall, forming with a windmill the touch of one N.M., whose initials are enclosed in an octagon; while 1641, according to the Rev. J. E. Nightingale's "Church Plate of Dorset," is the oldest date on pewter found in that county, viz., two flagons inscribed, " Ex dono Henrie Arnoldi Ilsingtoniensis."

The same year witnessed the passing of an Act by the Parliament of Scotland commanding every pewterer to mark his ware with the thistle, the Deacon's mark, and his own name, and ordaining that none but the finest pewter, such as in England bore the mark of the rose, was to be employed. It is probably owing to the regrettable carelessness displayed in preserving the records of the Hammermen of Glasgow that we find no mention of a pewterer in such as remain before 1648, for, though the now large and prosperous city was at that time but a small place, it had its cathedral, and it seems scarcely credible that there should have been no resident craftsmen to meet the demand that must have existed for the making and repairing of pewter ware. An unusual but significant employment for a member of the craft is revealed by an Act of Parliament passed at Edinburgh in 1649 to authorise the payment of a sum of four hundred and forty-six pounds odd sterling (five thousand three hundred and fifty-three Scots) due to one James Monteith from the Government for making musket and pistol balls, presumably for the Parliamentary forces in Scotland and England, two years before, an account which was duly discharged, thus saving the creditor from carrying out his rather Gilbertian threat of deserting his wife and family. Nor can James Monteith have been the only one among the pewterers to profit handsomely by the internal dissensions, for to his English contemporaries also it must have come as a not wholly disagreeable illustration of the old proverb anent an ill wind. As the long-drawn-out contest between King and Parliament dragged on its weary length, nobleman after nobleman and gentleman after gentleman sent his rich stores of gold and silver plate to be melted down to meet the endless drain upon the war-chest, and, since men must eat even in the intervals of victory and defeat,

OLD PEWTER

the vanished treasures were doubtless replaced by humble pewter. Even royalty itself, as we know, was fain at last to be content with such, for in the possession of Mrs. F. W. Barry there is a large and handsome rose-water dish, which was one of a set of six provided for the King's use when he lay at York. The opposing party in their turn also made much work for the pewterers' lathes and hammers, more especially when they flung out from the churches the fonts as savouring particularly of papistry, necessitating the use of pewter bowls and basins for baptismal purposes.

In France during this half-century the use of pewter—except the ornamental kind—by the nobility had steadily declined, and not even the permission given in 1650 to gild, silver, or lacquer it, forbidden till then save for church use, was successful in inducing them to return to it to any great extent, although by royal command, in order to defray the expenses of the endless wars, their plate was sent to the Mint, the King leading the way with "tables, candelabra, large seats of silver," so "enriched with figures, bas-reliefs, and chasings" that, though they had cost him ten million francs, the metal when melted down

Plate LXVIII

H. 10"

JUG, George IV

THE SEVENTEENTH CENTURY

was worth no more than three. So despised, indeed, had pewter become, that the Grande Mademoiselle when visiting Nanteuil six years later thought it needful to her dignity and delicate susceptibilities, while commending her supper, to deprecate the pewter it was served on.

The punishment recorded in 1652 of William Abernethie of Edinburgh for using bad metal, is remarkable as the only instance of such a necessity arising, a praiseworthy proof of the faithfulness with which the Incorporation and craftsmen fulfilled their obligations to the public.

It may, perhaps, be doubted whether the London Company was so unselfishly considerate for the consumer when in the same year it forbade Thomas Allen to lend his professional assistance to a Major Purling, who had invented a new material which he called Silvorum, and in the following year fined Lawrence Dyer for working in it, though the last, be it acknowledged, did aggravate his offence by selling it unmarked. One would like to know whether he paid any or all of his fine in the farthings stamped " $\frac{1}{4}$ of an ounce of fine pewter," which Cromwell found it necessary to issue that year in imitation of the tradesmen's tokens, which had for many years been fashioned in that material. Certainly it was on no sentimental, altruistic grounds that in 1658, when they were debarred from introducing their ware into Bordeaux, doubtless with its large wine trade a paying customer, the London pewterers grumbled, quite regardless of the fact that their own laws against the importation of foreign ware were of the strictest.

With the return of Charles II. to the throne in 1660 the hated yoke of Episcopalianism was again laid on the shoulders of the Church of Scotland, and doubtless a new era of melting down and refashioning church plate, pewter and otherwise, ensued; but the interests of the pewterers were not ignored, for in 1661 an Act was passed absolutely prohibiting the exportation of old pewter, a precaution by no means unnecessary if we may deduce the rarity of the metal there from the fact that it was estimated at nearly three times its value on the south side of the border. This high price, in fact, would seem to have had a damaging effect upon the business of the craftsmen, and to have driven those of Edinburgh into under-

THE SEVENTEENTH CENTURY

taking jobs outside their regular profession, for an Act was called for in 1663 to decide that plumbers belonged to a distinct trade, and that pewterers had no right to work in lead.

Cisterns and toys next appear among the articles fashioned of pewter in England, Mr. Samuel Pepys having purchased one of the former in 1667, while Francis Lea was fined ten shillings in 1668 for making the latter of inferior quality, for even to such small deer did the powerful Company deign to attend in the intervals of such weightier business as joining the Girdlers in 1669 in opposing the endeavour of the poor Crooked Lane men to get a charter for themselves, or, as in 1671, making puzzling and apparently contradictory resolutions as to the lawful use of the rose and crown stamp and the addition or omission of the name of the maker in full.

Pewter spoons and forks are found in a French inventory of 1672.

A series of ordinances issued by the Aberdeen Incorporation are interesting as showing with what intimate details of the daily life of its members, quite apart from their work, it was suffered to interfere. more especially in the case of apprentices, who, if the rules were conscientiously enforced, must have had a dull and rather difficult time. The quarrel between the pewterers and plumbers of Edinburgh came to a head next year, and resulted in 1679 in an action brought by the former in which they endeavoured to establish their right in the teeth of the Act of 1663 to work in lead, and some of the pleadings show the smallness of the trade, owing to which the craftsmen were unable to exist by it alone. Yet people of fair social standing did not hesitate to embark in it, a nephew of the Laird of Wallieford being apprenticed in 1687. The collapse of Episcopalianism and revival of Presbyterianism on the accession of William of Orange in 1688 led once again to alterations in church plate, though on this occasion much more of it was preserved intact, and some of it still survives.

In the course of the same year the pewterers of London made it clear that, however cordially they might welcome a king from foreign parts, they were not prepared to extend their toleration to rival workmen, for one Mark Henry Chabrolles, a Frenchman, was bluntly forbidden to open a "shopp.

PLATE LXIX

1 D. 5¾" 2 D. 4¼"
BARBER'S BOWL, English. TWO-HANDLED BOWL,
XVIII century. Dutch. XVIII century.

PLATE LXX

1 D. 6¼" Dep. 1¾" 2 D. 5" Dep. 2¼" 3 D. 6¼" Dep. 1¾"
PORRINGERS.

PLATE LXXI

1 L. 10¾"
BOWL, Scotch. Mark on one lug indecipherable.

2 H. 5½"
CASKET, French. XVI century. Marks in four shields: 1. Lion rampant ; 2. Cupid running ; 3 and 4. Unrecognisable.

3
BOWL. Marks crowned rose and W. R. W.

THE SEVENTEENTH CENTURY

Learning later that he was a Protestant refugee, they consented to his working "some time longer," but in 1692, repenting of its leniency, the Court finally ordered him to abandon the trade of pewterer by the 24th of August, as they recognised, somewhat tardily, that his practising it was illegal. At the same time it was tinkering with the rules as to stamping wares with a persistency and contrariety that would have rejoiced the heart of a War Office permanent official. In 1690 complaint was made that one Samuel Hancock was brazenly stamping his name in full upon his plates, yet in 1692 the Court ordered or allowed this to be done, only to renew its prohibition six months later, which was again withdrawn in 1697.

A significant entry appears in the records of Aberdeen for 1694 admitting white-iron-smiths to the freedom of the Incorporation, by which, as far as the pewterers were concerned, it was opening the gate to an insidious foe. Indeed, everywhere at the end of the seventeenth century signs of the approaching end of the prosperous days of the craft were becoming plainly visible. In Scotland the white-ironsmiths, in England the makers of glass and earthenware, were steadily absorbing more and more of the trade; so much so that the Pewterers' Company attempted, though in vain, to procure the passing of an Act of Parliament enforcing the sale on draught of beer and other intoxicating liquors in pewter vessels only, declaring with sublime effrontery that no others held full measure. It may even be doubted whether the long wars with France which followed the triumph of William of Orange and the final overthrow of the Stuarts gave much stimulus to the pewterers' trade, though William, after having been driven to the same expedients as his rival Louis XIV.—melting down the larger portion of the profusion of silver accumulated by Charles II., and calling on his subjects for similar sacrifices—was finally reduced to striking part of his coinage in pewter.

THE EIGHTH CHAPTER
THE END OF THE STORY

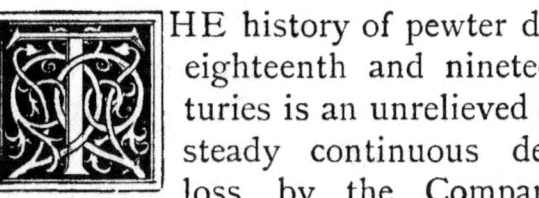THE history of pewter during the eighteenth and nineteenth centuries is an unrelieved record of steady continuous decline, of loss by the Companies and Incorporations of their power to control the trade, of loss finally by the craftsmen of the trade itself. At the beginning of the period the London Company was still struggling with the vexed question of the marking of pewter. Regulation after regulation had ordained that each maker should possess a mark peculiar to himself, that this mark should be registered on a plate kept for the purpose at the Company's Hall, and that every master should stamp this touch on every piece of pewter that issued from his shop. Yet in 1702 it was still necessary for the Company to obtain a charter empowering them to make more regulations, or rather to reiterate those that had been laid down so often before. The attempt to prevent the importation of foreign pewter would appear to have been no more

successful, in spite of the fact, as proved by a number of tests undertaken by the Company in 1709, that it was immensely inferior in quality to the native material.

In Scotland at the same period the insidious white-ironsmiths were gradually extending their boundaries. One is mentioned at Edinburgh in 1713; another, the first, was admitted as a freeman of the Dundee Incorporation in 1715; while—a still more significant fact—in 1720 the last pewterer, one Patrick Sampson of Dundee, joined the St. Andrews Incorporation.

The grip of the London Company weakened yearly. Few rules had been more persistently enforced than that forbidding anything approaching to self-advertisement, yet in 1727 one Samuel Smith had no hesitation in asserting publicly by means of the stamp upon his wares that these were "good mettle made in London." As far as the country was concerned matters were even worse. The Company, which had owned and regularly exercised the right of search for inferior ware throughout the length and breadth of England, though assured in 1729 that such was being offered for sale in large

PLATE LXXII

1 H. 5¾"
MUSTARD-POT, English.
XVII century.

2 H. 7"
HOT-WATER JUG, Dutch.
Early XVIII century.

3 H. 5¼"
MEASURE, English. Early
XVIII century.

PLATE LXXIII

1 D. 12″
WAVY-EDGED SALVER with feet. Dutch. Late XVIII century.

2 H. 9″
STUDENTS' BEER-JUG. German. XVII century.

3 D. 18″
DISH. English. XVIII century.

4 H. 6¼″
WATER-JUG. English. Late XVIII century.

5 D. 5¼″
WAVY-EDGED PLATE. English. Late XVIII century. One of a set of six.

THE END OF THE STORY

quantities at Bristol, no longer dared to put their prerogatives into practice, and by a timorous inaction surrendered their whole position and abandoned their justification for continued existence. To issue edicts to which, on your own confession, you have no means of compelling obedience, is to wilfully court humiliation. The weakness of the authorities was furthermore reflected in the trade itself. The makers lost their originality and individuality, and more and more as time went on we find them content merely to re-echo the work of the gold- and silver-smiths. This is especially observable in their table ware, as, for example, in the dish [Plate IX. 2], the mustard pots [Plates VII. 4, and VIII. 6 and 7], pepper pots [Plate VIII. 2 and 3], and salts [Plate VIII. 9 and 12], which, admirable as they are in design, are only slavish copies of the silver of the time.

In 1729 the last pewterer was enrolled among the Hammermen of the Cannongate, and, moreover, the Patrick Sampson who, as mentioned above, had migrated from Dundee to St. Andrews nine years previously, so evidently had found business in that city unsatisfactory that he shook its dust from his feet, and returning to his former place of residence sought and obtained admission to the Incorporation there, while the craftsmen of St. Andrews set themselves to the task of reducing the overcrowding of the Incorporation which had resulted from the ill-considered diminution of the entrance fees some years earlier, by enacting that no one who was not either the son of a freeman or married to the daughter of one should thenceforth be entitled to belong to it. How far this served to improve matters for the time we do not know, but in endeavouring to bolster up an out-of-date monopoly they were foredoomed to failure in the end. The spirit of the age, with its growing sense of personal freedom, was against all such galling restrictions on the liberty of the individual, however well directed to the public benefit they may have been, and from an order issued in 1732 to its members by the Incorporation of Perth to spy out what burgesses of the town were illegally trafficking with the unfreemen it is clear that the consumer from without was aiding and abetting the revolt from within. One by one the Incorporations had to retreat from positions formerly held in strength. Thus in 1733

THE END OF THE STORY

Patrick Campbell was admitted as freeman of both "the Coppersmith and the Pewter Arts," though only nine years earlier Ninian Grey, although Deacon of the Incorporation, was brought to book for working at the two. The same year the pewterers of Edinburgh, beginning, maybe, to realise their danger, endeavoured to assert their authority over the white-ironsmiths by denying them the right to alter without permission their "essay," as the test-pieces which a man had to make before admission to the freedom were called, but they had to give way, a result which might act, but did not, as a warning to their neighbours of the Cannongate, who, all unsuspecting, gave entrance to their first white-ironsmith that very year.

The London Company must have been equally ready to forego its lawful powers under continued pressure, or John Jupe would never have dared in 1736, not only to label his metal "Superfine," but to crown his defiance with the additional insult "French!"

By 1739 the white-ironsmiths of Edinburgh had waxed so fat in their own estimation that they began to kick, urging complaints against the pewterers and demanding the right to establish a definite and distinct craft of their own, but that time they went too far, and the pewterers firmly and successfully rejected the appeal. At Perth, in the course of the same year, a tinsmith, the first to be found in the records, actually appealed to the Incorporation for charitable relief, a disaster to one of the rival craft which should have afforded unbounded satisfaction to the pewterer members, and not the less so because George Brown, the beneficiary, had formerly been a pewterer and an officer of the Incorporation withal, and had deserted them for the enemy, evidently with very poor results as far as he was concerned. The year 1745, so fraught with bitter memories for Scotland, brought about a further reduction in the amount of any early plate yet remaining to the congregations of the disestablished, but not deserted, Episcopalian Church, whose members, naturally taking the side of the Pretender in the ill-fated attempt at rebellion, were ruthlessly harried by the victorious Duke of Cumberland, their plate being carried off and their chapels burned, though this in the upshot proved of some small benefit to the pewterers. For the

PLATE LXXIV

1. TANKARD, English, 4″ high. 2. DISH, Scotch, stamped with initials ADV and AW, century.
3. MUG WITH HANDLE, English, 5½″ high. 4. MEASURE, English, 2½″ high, 2¼″ diam. Early XVIII century. XVII century.
5. TANKARD, English, 4″ high. XVIII century. 6. TOBACCO-BOX, English, 5½″ high, 4″ diam. XVIII century.

PLATE LXXV

H. 12"
SOUP TUREEN, Russian. Archangel mark.

THE END OF THE STORY

congregations, impoverished and oppressed, could only afford the more modest ware when replenishing their ravaged stores, and as a consequence most of the Episcopalian pewter plate still in existence dates from the nearer side of " the Forty-five." This demand, however, was far too small to provide any serious check on the downward path of the doomed craft; in the very next year the Dundee Incorporation enrolled the last on its books, tinsmiths thenceforth occupying their places, while after 1747 no Perth Hammerman can be shown to have made a living out of pewter alone, combining the craft with work in copper or some other trade, a practice, as has been said, at one time utterly prohibited.

In London at the same time the Company, with an inability to recognise or an unwillingness to admit the hollowness of their pretensions which is almost pathetic, were still perseveringly legislating on the subject of touches, ordaining that all objects large enough should bear the Christian name and surname of maker or vendor, and smaller articles his registered mark, though their edicts were by then so openly disregarded that one Edward Box two years before, with apparently complete impunity, advertised by means of the stamp upon his ware that, in his opinion, there was " No better in London."

For the Episcopalians of Scotland we may well feel compassion in regard to the destruction of their ancient plate, since it was sacrificed nobly in a gallant if mistaken effort to uphold a falling cause, but for the Presbyterians, in their almost conspicuous lack of early vessels, we have nothing but contempt. Without compulsion, of their own foolish free will, they began to consider such precious relics as old-fashioned, and, from about the year 1750 onwards, remodelling silver plate and destroying pewter altogether they wrought their own devastation. Small wonder that the pewterers were dying out. The last was enrolled at Aberdeen in 1765, and at Perth in 1771, while at Glasgow by 1776 the white-ironsmiths were undisguisedly making numbers of articles which should have pertained properly to the pewterer. Nor do matters seem to have been any better abroad, for at Paris in 1776 the hitherto independent pewterers were joined in somewhat uncongenial union with the coppersmiths and scale-makers to form a single company. It was probably

THE END OF THE STORY

owing rather to the badness of trade in general than to any successful competition on the part of the pewterers that no white-ironsmith appears in the records of St. Andrews until 1787, for by 1794 the admissions of tinsmiths as compared with pewterers were as six to one, while those at Edinburgh in 1795 were strong enough to so far turn the tables as to secure the condemnation of a pewterer for undertaking their work. Well might the offender, James Wright, exclaim in bitterness, "Ichabod, Ichabod—thy glory has departed."

It would be a useless and ungrateful task to follow the practical extinction of the craft to the bitter end in the nineteenth century. The ever-increasing cheapness of glass and chinaware ousted pewter from table use, the discovery of the possibility of coating steel with tin, forming what is now known as block tin, introduced a material both stronger and lighter for hollow-ware, the invention of Britannia metal—a form indeed of pewter—German silver, nickel plate, and other compositions, either more silver-like in themselves or more easily susceptible to plating with silver, banished it for the most part from taverns and public eating-houses, and the isolation of zinc as a distinct metal and its employment in combination in the form of galvanised iron gave a result more convenient for many and varied domestic and commercial purposes. To complete the downfall, the pewterers themselves made no effort to meet the altering conditions. With that fine British conservative obstinacy which is by no means extinct as yet among us, they declined to adapt their ancient methods to new demands. They adhered resolutely to the good old principle, which has exercised such unmistakable effects upon our foreign trade that it is the business of the customer to want what the manufacturer chooses to make, in no way whatever that of the manufacturer to make what the customer wants, and, clinging with limpet-like consistency to the rock of trade traditions, they let the tide of public requirements ebb away from them, never to return. The last touch on the plates at Pewterer's Hall is dated 1824, and though the Company still survives, and is by no means the smallest or poorest among its fellows, its official purpose is non-existent. A Mr. James Moyes kept a pewterer's shop in the West Bow, Edinburgh, until some time

PLATE LXXVI

1 D. 7″
VEGETABLE DISH.
English. Late XVIII
century.

2 9 × 13½″
TRAY or SALVER,
Dutch.

3 H. 4″
MILK JUG,
English.
Late XVIII
century.

4 H. 8″
WATER JUG, English.
XVIII century.

Plate LXXVII

Ewer H. 8¾" Basin, 14" × 10¾"

EWER AND BASIN.

THE END OF THE STORY

between 1870 and 1880, though it it is said that for some years previously he had ceased the manufacture. The Incorporations of Hammermen at Aberdeen, Dundee, Perth, and Stirling still hold meetings and make a poor pretence of carrying on their business, but as they possess no executive powers the practical effect is insignificant; indeed, as far as pewter is concerned, is nil. Some little pewter is still made in London on the old lines, and there are even now eating-houses where, with a pleasant if somewhat artificial conservatism, the guest is served on pewter, but the recent attempts to revive the craft by bending it to the too often ill-directed purposes of the so-called new art have not as yet produced much calling for extended notice.

THE NINTH CHAPTER
COLLECTING AND DISPLAYING PEWTER

N the matter of a scientific knowledge of his chosen subject founded on accurate and organised information the collector of pewter is, and most indisputably will always remain, sadly at a disadvantage in comparison with the collector of gold and silver plate. In theory, had the regulations of the Companies and Incorporations been rigorously enforced or loyally adhered to, and had the records been faithfully kept and carefully preserved, there should have been no more difficulty in establishing the identity of the maker of any specimen and ascertaining its approximate date in the one case than in the other. Every article would have borne the touch of the craftsman. A comparison of this with the touch-plate and a consultation of the register of touches and of the list of freemen would have been all that was necessary for full enlightenment. Unfortunately this ideal state of things is very far from

PLATE LXXVIII

1 D. 14″
BOWL. Flemish. XVII century.

2 H. 10″
JUG. Dutch. Early XVIII century.

PLATE LXXIX

1	2	3	4	5
H. 3½″ D. 2¼″ MUSTARD-POT. XVIII century.	H. 2½″ D. 2¾″ SALT-CELLAR. XVIII century.	H. 2″ D. 2½″ MUSTARD-POT. Late XVIII century.	H. 4½″ Base 2″ PEPPER-BOX. XVIII century.	H. 2½″ D. 3″ MEASURE. XVIII century.

PLATE LXXX

From 4″ to 6″ high

MUSTARD-POTS.   XVII and XVIII centuries.

PLATE LXXXI

From 4½″ to 6″ high

PEPPER-POTS.   XVII and XVIII centuries

COLLECTING AND DISPLAYING

prevailing. In practice it may be said that it is the exception rather than the rule when this is possible. Indeed, it would probably be no exaggeration to assert that nine out of ten of the existing specimens of pewter bear no mark at all, and that of those which are marked ninety-nine out of every hundred now convey no intelligible meaning. There are indeed, as has been previously observed, five plates of touches at Pewterers' Hall, and Mr. Masse has patiently described every touch upon them, but the registers which should have preserved the names of their owners have disappeared, and the result in the present state of our knowledge is only useful to a limited extent. The number of these touches is nearly twelve hundred, but of these only forty-one give the name and date. In the case of two hundred and fifty the name alone is recorded, but, as the same is included in the list of freemen also reproduced by Mr. Masse, we may, in the majority of them, arrive with fairly assured certainty at the period at which the vessel so marked was made, while in three instances the date is given and the name may be conjectured. In no less than three hundred and six instances, on the other hand, the name on the touch is not to be found in the list of freemen; in one hundred and fifty-six a date, with initials or a device, is all the information afforded, and in all the remaining cases there is neither name nor date to guide us. The authorities, in fact, as long as their power was paramount, did all they could to baffle the collector of the future, unconsciously, of course, for it can never have occurred to craftsmen, working their best, indeed, but with no deliberate artistic intent, that posterity would take any interest in their productions, but none the less effectively, since these dateless initials and nameless devices may be traced directly to their horror of self-advertisement and their consequent prohibition of a touch bearing name or address, even so wide a one as "London" having been for long forbidden.

Had the touches only been put upon the plates in orderly succession we should have been less at a loss, for it would at all events have been possible to assign a date to a touch lacking one somewhere between the nearest previous and succeeding ones which were dated; but there is no doubt whatever that

PLATE LXXXII

1 H. 3", CREAM-JUG, Scotch.
2 L. 7¼"
3 H. 2", SALT-CELLAR, English. Cromwellian.
4 L. 7¼"
5 H. 2¾", SALT-CELLAR, English.
6 L. 6¼"
7 H. 2", SALT-CELLAR, English. Georgian.
8 L. 6¼"
9 H. 1¾", ¼ GILL MEASURE, Glasgow mark.
10 L. 7"

DUTCH SPOONS.

COLLECTING AND DISPLAYING

no system was followed, but that the striker chose his own place haphazard, left his mark where he would, and actually, to a certain extent, made choice of what plate he would strike it on. In no other way can we account for the fact that the earliest remaining plate bears such dates as 1679, 1680, 1687, &c., though the second shows 1676, and the fourth plate was stamped in 1704, 1705, and so on, while the third contains one as late as 1786, and many others of the later half of that century. Nor is this the last of the sources of possible confusion. Makers sometimes marked their wares with a touch differing from the one on the touch-plate, and this not only in those cases where, as a penalty for infringing some regulation, or for other good reason, one was ordered to change his touch, duly recording the new one. Thus Tim Fly, who was Warden in 1737 and Master in 1739, and should therefore have been staunch in upholding the rules of the Company, registered his name and a punning device of a fly as his distinguishing mark, yet a specimen in the collection of Mr. Hugh Bryan bears his name and a cock and crown, which is not to be found on the touch-plates, together with the forbidden four small stamps simulating the hall-marks on gold or silver plate. Finally, to crown our uncertainty, some makers, either illegally and probably with fraudulent intent, or with due permission given on sufficient grounds, used the touch registered by another man, while some provincial pewterers, as, for instance, one Stephen Maxwell, of Glasgow, went so far as to stamp "London" on their home-made goods, doubtless to enhance the price. These Edinburgh touches, as far as they go, are much more instructive than those of London, as a large majority of the one hundred and twenty-nine described by Mr. Wood are dated between 1600 and 1764, and in a great number of cases it has been possible, with more or less certainty, to connect the initials on them with a contemporary name in the existing lists of freemen and apprentices. Unfortunately only two of these touch-plates or counterpanes survive, and they, it would seem, by a happy and mysterious accident. Whether the Incorporations of the other Scottish cities kept their own touch-plates, as York, in England, did, is not known. Probably they did, as

COLLECTING AND DISPLAYING

they certainly made regulations as to touches, but in no instance has any been preserved. With regard to private touches, then, the owner of any vessel bearing one would be well advised to search through the lists given by Mr. Massé and Mr. Wood on the chance of identifying it, though the likelihood of his doing so, or of obtaining any great accession of knowledge if he does so, cannot be said to be very great. Speaking broadly, and with due regard to exceptions, we may infer from Mr. Masse's list that up to the end of the seventeenth century the proportion of stamps bearing names to those bearing initials and devices was small, that names in full increase constantly in frequency during the eighteenth century, and that by the end of it the use of initials alone had almost died out.

In respect to the general marks which every pewterer was supposed to use, matters are not in a much more satisfactory condition. The rose or the **X**, crowned or uncrowned, were English guarantees of quality at an early date, but the former was sometimes used under pretence of being a private touch on inferior ware, and in the eighteenth century it was adopted without any

OLD PEWTER

such meaning as it had in the south by many pewterers in Scotland. A similar mark also occurs on pewter of the second quality made at Liége, and on ware from Ghent, Nuremberg, and many other places in Holland, Flanders, and Germany. The **x,** whether crowned or not, denoting extraordinary ware, and four small marks imitating those on silver plate, were frequent in London from at least the beginning of the seventeenth century in spite of the energetic protests of the Goldsmiths, but these also were adopted in Scotland during the eighteenth century, while the thistle, which after 1641 was an evidence of good material in Scotland, was sometimes used by English makers, possibly Scotsmen naturalised, in their private touches. A crowned hammer was a mark used at Mons as early as 1467, sometimes accompanied by the word "fin," and the same mark, without the word, of course, was used as a sign of first quality in Scotland during the sixteenth century. The *fleur-de-lys* was the mark of third quality at Liége, but was also often used in France, and the same was, by an order made in 1548, to be stamped on the lids attached in London to stoneware or

PLATE LXXXIII

1	2 D. 4⅛"	3 H.5¾"	4	5
MEASURE	SALT.	SUGAR-CASTOR.	VINEGAR CRUET.	INKSTAND.

PLATE LXXXIV

SALTS.   1 H. 1¾"   2 H. 1½"   3 H. 2"   4 H. 2"   5 H. 2⅛"

COLLECTING AND DISPLAYING

earthenware pots on the outside to begin with, though in 1559 it was, for some obscure reason, transferred to the inside. Not even "London" or "Made in London" can be accepted as absolute evidence of provenance, as has been remarked before. The castle of Edinburgh, though by no means invariably present, seems a fairly certain mark of nationality, but may possibly be confused with the castle used at Mons, and the double eagle and half eagle between the flails of Nuremberg appear to have been almost the only marks that were not duplicated elsewhere.

When pewter bearing a mark affords such shifting and uncertain footing to the inquirer, it is small wonder that it should present a very quagmire of doubt and hesitation when it is entirely without mark of any kind, and this is only too commonly the case. In the excellent illustrated "Catalogue of the Pewter Exhibition," organised by Mr. Massé at Clifford's Inn Hall in 1904, the words "Maker's mark none" or an equally expressive silence occur again and again. Out of fifty-nine vessels still existing in twenty-nine churches in the Diocese of

OLD PEWTER

Llandaff, as recorded in Mr. J. E. Halliday's published "Terrier," only fifteen are marked, and the list of evidences to the same effect might be almost indefinitely extended, but every collector of pewter knows how greatly unmarked specimens preponderate. The reasons are not far to seek, and, though in the main conjectural, are not without considerable antecedent probability. In the first place, though the gold- and silver-smiths were compelled to carry their finished wares to the Company's Hall, where they were assayed and stamped by the proper officials, while any evasion, owing to the intrinsic value of the material, would certainly be pointed out by the purchaser and promptly and severely punished, the pewterer was, in most cases, allowed to mark his wares in his own shop, subject always to surprise visits by the Company's searcher, and as the customer would doubtless be less particular as to the exact quality of this cheaper metal, avoidance of the obligatory marks must have been much easier. In the second place, it is certain that the use of pewter would have lingered on in the remoter country districts for many years after it had gone out of

PLATE LXXXV

| 1 L. 6" | 2 | 3 H. 5" | 4 H. 2⅝" | 5 H. 5¾" | 6 H. 2¼" |

SUGAR-SIFTERS.   SET OF CRUETS. Scotch.   SPIRIT-LAMP
XVIII century.   XVIII century.

PLATE LXXXVI

| 1 H. 4" | 2 H. 5⅜" | 3 H. 1½" | 4 H. 5¼" | 5 H. 4¼" |

CREAM-JUG   HERB-CAN-   BOX. No   HERB-CAN-   CREAM-JUG,
Scotch. No   NISTER.   mark.   NISTER. Dutch.   No mark.
mark.   Dutch. XVII   Marked 1766, a
        century. Mark   Cupid in profile
        a standing   blowing a horn.
        figure.   P.S.B.

PLATE LXXXVII

1 H. 14½"
DUTCH URN.

2 H. 16"
FRENCH URN. XVIII century.

3 H. 15"
DUTCH URN.

COLLECTING AND DISPLAYING

fashion in London and other large towns, while the London Company lost control over the provincial makers long before their authority ceased to be effective in the City. Furthermore, even when their powers theoretically extended over the whole of England we know that tinkers, gypsies, and other travelling pewterers went about the country melting down and re-casting worn-out pewter in spite of frequently renewed edicts against them, so that in the course of a century or two very little, if any, of the ware can have retained its original form and markings. Now it is highly unlikely that these unlicensed workers whom the Company was so ceaselessly, though vainly, endeavouring to suppress would have stamped any mark which might lead to their identification on their wares, nor would the employer be keen in demanding such, and as a very large proportion of the old pewter, which, now that the demand for it is growing, is finding its way into the market, comes from these rural districts, the general lack of marks is in no way surprising.

This conclusion, if held valid, compels us to the recognition of yet another stumbling-block in the path of a collector anxious to date his pewter, for these pedlars working, as they did, surreptitiously in constant fear of detection, and in a necessarily small way, would not have been able, even if they could have afforded, to procure a constant supply of new moulds, nor could they well have carried about with them an extensive variety of such bulky and ponderous objects without attracting undesirable attention from the authorities of any town they passed through, and it follows that their productions, in most, if not in all cases, must have been antiquated in style to an unascertainable extent. In the absence of marks, however, style is practically the only indication of time and place of manufacture, and when it is probable, considering the durability of the massive metal moulds, that in remote country neighbourhoods vessels were being turned out in shapes a century or more perhaps behind the prevailing taste in London, an element of uncertainty to a quite incalculable amount is introduced into all such deductions. Nevertheless uncertainty is preferable to absolute ignorance, and, keeping well in mind this possible source of error, we must continue to judge the period of a vessel

PLATE LXXXVIII

1 H. 7″ D. 5″
TEAPOT. Early XIX century.

2 H. 4″ D. 2¼″
CREAM-JUG. Early XIX century.

3 H. 4¾″ D. 3¼″
COFFEE-POT. XVIII century.

PLATE LXXXIX

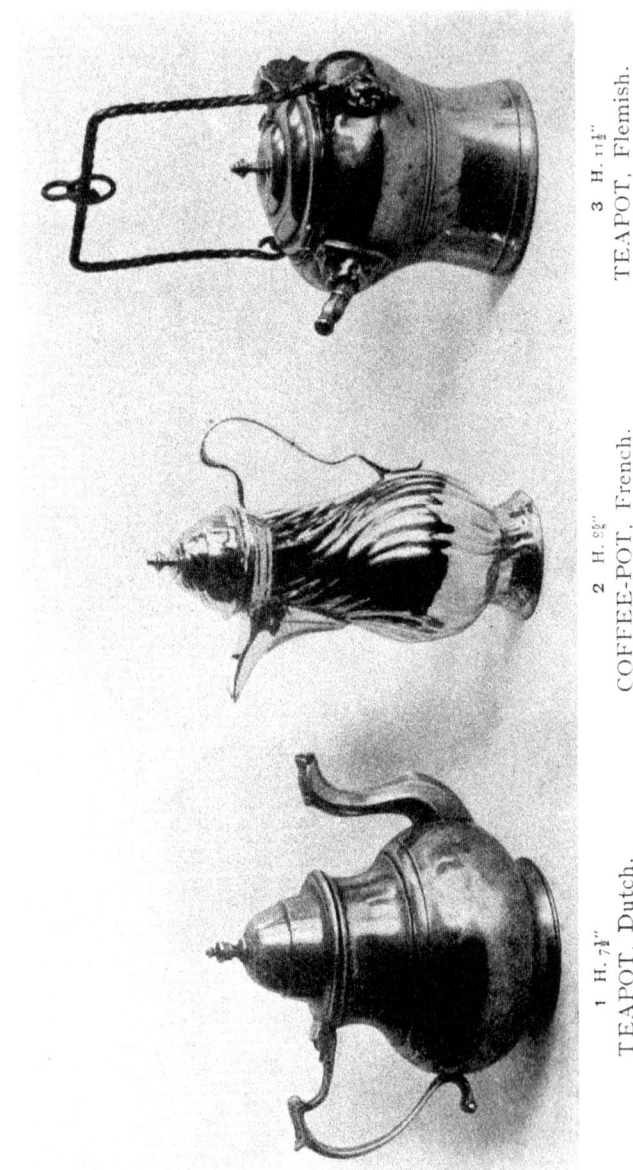

1 H. 7½"
TEAPOT, Dutch.
XVIII century.

2 H. 9⅝"
COFFEE-POT, French.
XVIII century.

3 H. 11¼"
TEAPOT, Flemish.
XVIII century.

COLLECTING AND DISPLAYING

from its form. There is much yet to be done in accumulating and codifying the necessary materials even for this, and only vague and general indications can as yet be attempted, taking the form rather of rough and detached notes than of any connected story of development. No hard-and-fast dogmatic propositions can be accepted. Speaking only generally, then, and taking as understood the "possibly's" and "perhaps's" with which every paragraph should bristle if we would keep strictly within the four corners of allowable hypothesis, we may venture to assume that the greater the simplicity the greater the age. Straight or slightly waved lines preceded swelling curves, flat unadorned lids came before domed tops with knobs or crests, few and simple mouldings were the forerunners of many and elaborate ones. This decorative evolution as displayed in the thumb-pieces of tavern-measures made in Scotland is effectively described and illustrated by Mr. Wood in the volume so often quoted before, and at the same time he lays down various broad rules of the greatest importance to the collector. For example: that a vessel with the lower part of the handle attached directly to the

OLD PEWTER

body is older than one in which it is connected with it by a short intervening peg or strut; that the Scottish "quaigh" differs from the porringer, so often incorrectly called a bleeding-vessel or barber's bowl, by the fact that the first was round-bottomed, the second flat, and that the handles or "lugs" were always plain and solid, not pierced or otherwise ornamented; that the older a plate is the broader is the rim and the thicker the metal of which it is made, though this refers chiefly, if not wholly, to large plates; that, owing to the national partiality for broth, porridge, and other more or less fluid foods, their plates were generally deeper than those used in England; and that up to 1707, and less regularly up to 1835, the Scots measures differed conspicuously from the English, the former being the Scots gill, which was eight-tenths of the English gill, the mutchkin, which held three English gills, the chopin, containing one pint two gills English measure, the Scots pint, familiarly known as a "Tappit-hen" [Plate X. 2], a peculiarly characteristic type of vessel which equalled three of the degenerate English pints, and the noble Scots gallon, which absorbed three petty English ones; while in

COLLECTING AND DISPLAYING

his two chapters on " Church vessels before and after the Reformation," he provides a wealth of information as to the various shapes which these assumed at different periods, and the distinctive features of those appertaining to the Presbyterian and Episcopalian forms of worship respectively. In considering style and estimating from it the probable date of pewter ware, a knowledge of the contemporary work of the gold- and silver-smiths will be found of the greatest assistance. It is certain that the pewterers were accustomed to follow with considerable closeness the designs in favour with them, doubtless at the instigation of their customers, who desired that their table furnishing, though cheap, should be in the mode. More especially would this seem to have been the case with Church plate, and naturally enough only those parishes which were too poor to afford better would content themselves with the baser and doubtfully canonical material, and they would have been more than human had they not done their best to conceal from stranger eyes the narrowness of their circumstances. To this desire to keep up appearance, quite as much as to a sense of the sacredness of the vessels, may perhaps be ascribed the precise rules as to "scouring" it which were in force, one of which, quoted from Boissonet by Bapst, some collector may be inclined to try. "It must be washed every three months in hot soap-suds, and be rubbed with oats or other husk-bearing grain, or with broken egg-shells; then washed in clean water, dried, and wiped with a clean cloth."

Thanks to the inclusion in the hall-marks on gold or silver plate of a letter definitely denoting the year of manufacture, it is, as a rule, easy to fix the date of these, and it will be a fairly safe presumption that pewter in the same fashion is of somewhat later make. Coats-of-arms engraved upon it may also at times afford indications of the date, though these must always be regarded with some suspicion. Even if genuine there can be no assurance that they have not been added later, while there is only too good reason to suspect that the forging of them is becoming a common practice among some unscrupulous dealers.

To the young collector anxious for certain guiding in the subject he has selected it is to be feared the foregoing remarks will prove

PLATE XC

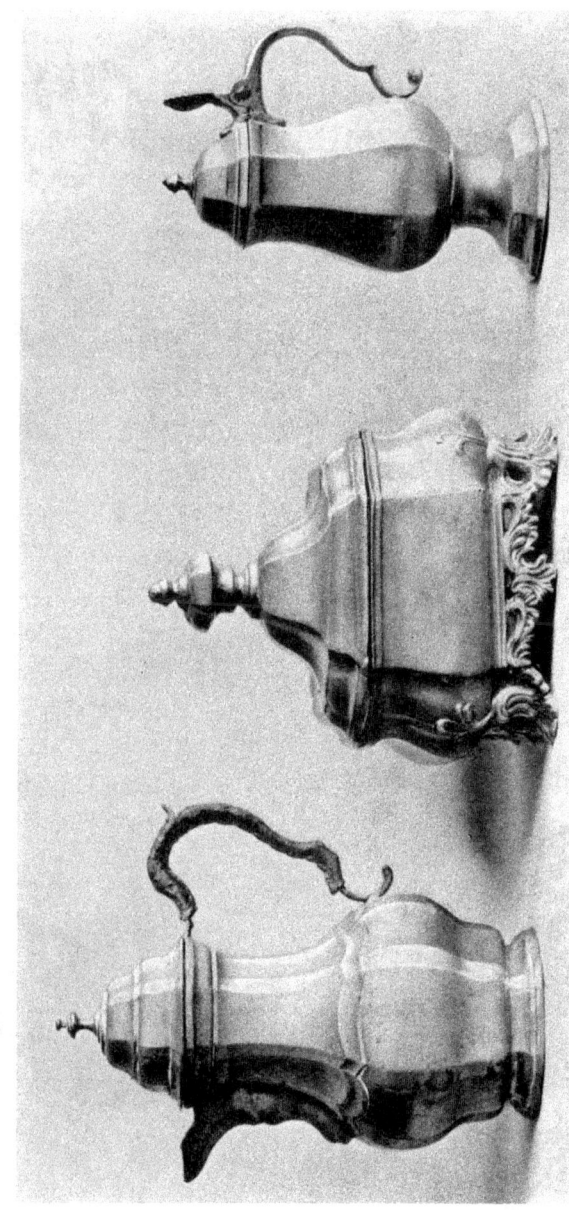

1 H. 7"
COFFEE-POT. Louis XIV style German. First half of XVIII century.

2 H. 6"
SUGAR-BOX AND COVER, Dutch. Dated 1751. Given by J. H. Fitzhenry, Esq.

3 H. 5¼"
MUSTARD-POT. Marked with a figure floating in the air.

PLATE XCI

1   2   3
EGG-CUPS, no marks.
4   5   6 H. 2¼" 7   8   9
SET OF SIX EGG-CUPS, Scotch. No marks.

PLATE XCII

1 H. 3½"   2 H. 2" D. 3"   3 H. 6¼"
MILK-JUG, English. SUGAR-BASIN, TEAPOT, English. Early
Early XIX century. English. Early XIX century.
XIX century.

COLLECTING AND DISPLAYING

not a little disappointing, but to such a one it may be suggested that it is to the gradual increase of knowledge accruing from it that one of the highest pleasures of forming a collection is due. He who buys wholesale, relying solely on the dictum of the dealer or the authority of the expert, without attempting to arrive at any opinion founded on his own judgment, misses one of its chiefest joys. It is better to make a few mistakes, provided that these are not too costly, and to profit by them, than to depend in ignominious ignorance upon the real or assumed experience of another, however inglorious a security this may by chance result in. If he does not appreciate the simple beauties of good pewter no one is likely to be tempted to possess it, and if an object displays this unaffected beauty to its owner's eyes it is not a matter of very great importance to what century exactly it may belong, always presuming that its alleged date has not been made the excuse for extorting a purely fancy price.

In conclusion a few lines may be devoted to indicating briefly some of the articles in pewter which the collector may hope to find, although it would be tedious to attempt a complete catalogue of the uses to which it was applied. Plates and dishes, flagons and tankards, measures and drinking vessels of diverse forms and sizes are comparatively common, as are candlesticks, inkstands, porringers, bowls and basins of various sorts; while among the less frequent objects are articles of church plate, lavers, chalices, patens, baptismal bowls, fonts, and so on, guild cups from foreign cities, salt-cellars, pepper and mustard pots, tobacco and snuff-boxes, candle boxes, tea-caddies, lamps, some with glass reservoirs and a divided band indicating the hour's consumption of oil for night use, spoons and forks, Scotch communion tokens, beggars', porters' and other badges, tea and coffee pots, punch ladles, colanders, powder-puff boxes, and money-boxes, eggstands, haggis-dishes, and quaighs. The seeker after pewter has no need to fear monotony in his pursuit.

When the collection has been made or has, at any rate, attained a sufficient importance in quantity and quality, the question of its disposition so as to display its decorative powers and æsthetic features in the most complete and characteristic manner becomes one for serious consideration. Beyond all

COLLECTING AND DISPLAYING

question the happiest results are secured in those few but fortunate cases where in old country houses the vessels made for and used by departed ancestors remain in their original habitation, either still spread out on the very shelves and dressers primarily designed to receive them or removed with loving care into equally congenial but more generally accessible surroundings. This, however, may be rapidly passed over as an usually unattainable counsel of perfection. The principle, nevertheless, is one that should be borne carefully in mind when the subject of arrangement calls for attention. It must never for one moment be forgotten that, leaving out of account the highly ornamented but artistically wrong works of Briot, Enderlein, and the like, the prime intention of pewter was practical, every-day usefulness, that the beauties it possesses are incidental rather than intentional, arising from the perfection of its construction and adaptation to purpose, and that consequently any setting that tends in any way to weaken or destroy the clear impression of its maker's meaning will be *ipso facto* a bad one. In short, though devoting it in reality solely to purposes of ornament, we should endeavour to retain a suggestive reminiscence of possible use.

One cannot, of course, dogmatically predicate the hidden influences working on another's mind, but one may tentatively assume that like effects, as a rule, spring from like causes, and deduce from that postulate a belief that few, if any, true lovers of pewter are blind altogether to the large part which associations play in the fostering of their devotion. It is out of its very homeliness that pewter weaves one of its most potent spells. From the world at large crowned heads and belted earls are too far removed to greatly stir the imagination. The gorgeous gold and silver of royal feasts and noble revels, flashing beneath the electric lamps, dazzle more than they delight. The modest, moonlight sheen of pewter, on the other hand, blinking demurely on the oak dresser in the dancing firelight of a winter's night, speaks to us of ourselves. We may trace it back in fancy to the shelves of some stout and prosperous burgher, long since crumbled into dust beneath some silent city church, to the stone-paved house-place of some far-off farm-house, at the highest to

PLATE XCIII

1 H. 5¾″   2 H. 5½″

TEAPOT, English. Early XIX century.   TANKARD, English. XVIII century.

PLATE XCIV

1   H. 5" D. 4   2   H. 4" D. 4"   3   H. 4"
TEAPOT. Early XIX century.   TEAPOT. XVIII century.   TOBACCO BOX. XVIII
                                                                    century.

COLLECTING AND DISPLAYING

some comfortable country manor inhabited by well-to-do gentry, for we prefer to keep aloof from the clattering scullions in the kitchens of the great. Or giving looser reins to the Pegasus of our musings as the glowing coals fall together and the flames leap up anew, we may more definitely conceive our mind-pictures, and bring into them well-known figures from the distant past. That measure may have stood upon the board between Shakespeare and Ben Jonson at the Mermaid Tavern; from that tankard Marlowe may have supped his last draught before the footman's sword brought to nothing his mighty if erratic genius; Dicky Steele may have taken that candlestick in his shaky hand to re-light his oft-extinguished pipe; and why should not Robby Burns have filled a mug from that "Tappit-hen?"

But to feel certainly that these agreeable pictures are provable facts, we must have our pewter in congenial surroundings. It cannot be denied, indeed, that to an owner who fully realises its limitations as well as its capabilities, pewter is to no small extent exacting in its demands. It possesses so marked an individuality, so large a measure

OLD PEWTER

of dignity and solidity, that it will combine harmoniously with few of the ordinary embellishments of the average house. No one, it may be taken for granted, would dream of enshrining it in the fanciful glass cases or on the delicate velvet-covered shelves and niches of a drawing-room, or of forcing it into incongruous propinquity to the dainty subtleties of Dresden china or Venetian glass. Such a proceeding would be too flagrantly absurd; yet, setting aside such extremes of bad judgment, it is not difficult, with the best intentions, to fall into error nearly as serious; and complete success will, in most cases, be found in keeping it apart in, as far as possible, conditions approximating in their simplicity to what may not inaptly be termed natural. We cannot all command for it stone floors, wood panelling and antique furniture; nor ought we to expect, even if we could, any one but an enthusiast so far to sacrifice comfort to æsthetic appropriateness; but we may at least spare it the indignity of an anachronistic connection with gilded gimcracks and modern wall-papers. The charm of well-wrought and well-designed pewter lies, in the main, in form and colour, and the

COLLECTING AND DISPLAYING

fullest expression of these should be the sole aim. Isolation, and the carefully considered but not too obviously intentional combination of sufficiently numerous examples, will most surely secure the desired result. Plates, dishes, and other shallow objects may be arranged effectively and justifiably on shelves or ledges of proportionate apparent strength in passages or ante-rooms, the wood being either naturally dark or stained, and the background of some uniform light tint, undisturbed by fretful patterns, in harmony with the general tone of the material. In the selection of this there is ample scope for personal preferences, though it will be found that plain, unpretentious whitewash is hard to beat. Never, under any circumstances, should a specimen be suspended in any way. A porcelain plate seemingly adherent to the wall is ridiculous enough; a pewter plate under such inane conditions is an eyesore. More bulky objects, jugs, tankards, and so on, backed by plates and dishes in goodly array, will find a fitting home in the dining-room, and the trouble and expense will be abundantly repaid by the enhanced beauty of the exhibit if an old oak or walnut dresser is secured for their reception, and smaller hollow-ware, mugs, porringers, &c., are hung on hooks along the front edges of the shelves. These, with candlesticks, snuff-boxes, and the endless variety of smaller articles, may also be well disposed upon the mantelpiece and on shelves over it; always, however, taking good care that none are placed too high above the level of the eye, that the examples are neither so widely dispersed as to suggest specimens in a museum nor so crowded together as to interfere with the spectator's full enjoyment of the lines and curves of each individual object; and lastly, that the illumination shall be as full as can be managed, for the colour of pewter is of a delicate nature, and in a dim light it is apt to take on a dull and leaden hue.

The final steps before installing the collection in its destined place are the cleaning and the repairing, as far as is desirable, the effects of time and ill-usage. As to the extent to which the former process may legitimately be carried there may be no little difference of opinion. Undoubtedly, when the objects first came fresh and fair from the maker's workshop they were as bright as

PLATE XCV

1 H. 6¼″   2 H. 7⅜″   3 6¼″
COFFEE-POT. Flemish.   INKSTAND. French.   TOBACCO-BOX. French.
XVIII century.   XVIII century.   XVIII century.

PLATE XCVI

1 L. 2⅜"
SNUFF-BOX. No marks. XVIII century.

2 L. 2¾"
A PAIR OF SHOE BUCKLES. The forks of hand-cut steel. No marks.

3 L. ¼"
SNUFF-BOX. No marks.

4 W. 1¾"

5 D. 1⅜"
SNUFF-BOX. Scotch. No marks.

PLATE XCVII

1 H. 5" 2 H. 3¾"
PEPPER-POTS, English. XVIII century. Early XIX century.

3 H. 3¼"
MUSTARD-POT, English. Early XVIII century.

4 L. 3¼"
SNUFF-BOX English. Middle XVIII century.

5 H. 2¼"
EGG-CUP, with bead pattern, English XVIII century.

PLATE XCVIII

1 H. 4¼"
INK-POT, Scotch. No mark.

2 H. 2"
INKSTAND, Italian. With ink-holder, sand-box, holes for two quills, and drawer for wafers.

3 H. 2¼"
TOBACCO-BOX. No marks.

COLLECTING AND DISPLAYING

silverware, and it cannot be denied that a well-chosen display, cleaned and polished to the highest point of brilliancy, is an attractive sight. Yet, on the other hand, one cannot altogether unreluctantly destroy the results of the mellowing hand of time, and the problem would seem, on the whole, one of those that is best left to individual predilection for solution. It may, however, be remarked that, according to Mr. Gowland, the Japanese, whose supreme attainments in subtleties of taste Western nations have long since learned to acknowledge, never attempt to clean or polish pewter after it has left the fashioner's hands, confining themselves to an occasional rubbing with a piece of silk or cotton. The result of this is that the various slightly differing alloys which, as has already been pointed out, develop during the process of cooling acquire somewhat different tones in the course of the slow oxidisation which they undergo when exposed to the air, and the consequent mottling of a light and darker patina, when well marked and evenly distributed, is a highly valued and much appreciated feature of the ware.

With regard to repairs, unless these are

absolutely necessary it is better as a general rule to refrain from the attempt, but if such must be undertaken the judicious lover of his pewter will be at the slight pains of learning to execute them himself. The use of a blow-pipe and soldering-iron for patching up holes and rents, though calling for differences of manipulation under differing circumstances, and not easy therefore to make clear in words, is not in actual practice difficult to acquire. A few experiments on objects of no importance will soon lead to dexterity, and the owner of some neatly mended treasure will feel himself well rewarded should he subsequently encounter in some rival collection the ghastly results of confiding such a delicate operation to the clumsy mercies of the average British workman. For the dents, which few hollow vessels altogether escape in the chances and changes of life, pressure applied artfully, and above all very gently and gradually, inside with the round knob of a poker, the head of a curtain-pole, or even a wooden spoon will usually be found effectual, but in more obstinate cases it may be needful, after placing a hard object of the right shape

COLLECTING AND DISPLAYING

inside, to beat very lightly with a curved-faced hammer outside all round the circumference of the bulge, which, if done with caution will eventually restore it to its former level. Slight scratches are easily removed by rubbing with fine emery-powder, but no attempt should be made to eradicate the deeper knife-cuts which will generally be found on plates and dishes that have been much used. It is not, after all, advisable to endeavour to render old pewter indistinguishable from new.

In the case of the irregular black blotches and stains caused by oxidisation, which invariably occur upon examples—often the richest prizes—which have been brought to light, forgotten and long-neglected, from the obscure recesses of a broker's shop or country cottage, a long soaking in paraffin is the surest and safest remedy, for, though it may be done more rapidly by a careful treatment with acids, the process is not without its inconveniences, not to speak of dangers to hands and garments.

Finally, when all that is needed has been done, and supposing there is no intention of using the ware, as will most often be the case, a very thin coating of oil, or still better, vaseline, applied to the entire surface of each specimen will form an admirable protection against the effects of the atmosphere, and will greatly reduce the frequency of necessary cleanings.

PLATE XCIX

1 H. 8¾″ FLAGON. XVII century.
2 H. 5″ INKSTAND. Late XVIII century.
3 H. 8⅜″ FLAGON. XVII century.

PLATE C

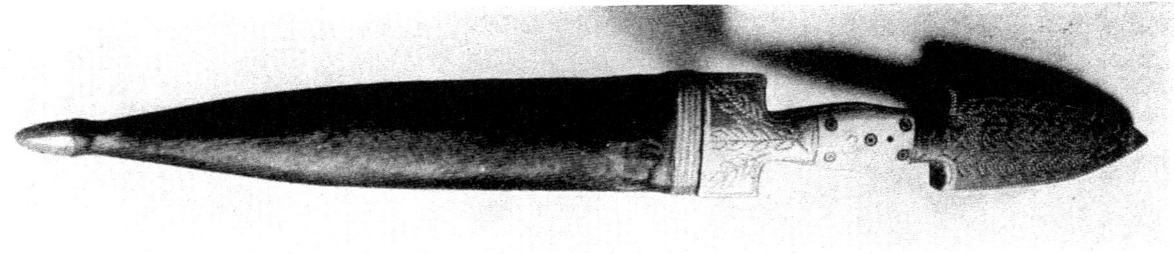

L. 74. ORIENTAL DAGGER. Handle of pewter and bone. Top and bottom of sheath bound with pewter. No marks.

THE TENTH CHAPTER

SOME NOTES ON THE ILLUSTRATIONS

FORKS AND SPOONS

THESE are the forms in which we most seldom find pewter at the present day. Indeed the first are the very rarest of all objects. When gathering specimens for the Exhibition at Clifford's Inn, Mr. Massé was only able to secure a single fork, and an inspection of many collections made for the purpose of selecting the materials for the illustration of this volume only revealed one further example. Nor is this scarcity in any way surprising. It is not probable that forks were made in any great quantity in so unsuitable a metal. Strength and sharpness are the fundamental qualities required in the prongs of a fork, and neither could be assured permanently in so soft a medium. The points would very soon get blunt, and the necessary slenderness of the various parts would quickly lead, under even fair wear and tear, to

breakage. The one we reproduce in the middle of Plate XI. 2 is small and exquisitely finished with well-designed ornament, and may perhaps have once formed part of a dessert service, to which use alone pewter might be applicable, but it seems more probable that it is in fact one of those trial pieces which the goldsmiths and silversmiths are known to have made in pewter.

Spoons, though decidedly less exceptional, are very far from common. The thinness of the stem and the inevitable point of weakness at the junction of this with the bowl rendered them very liable to damage under rough usage, while the small quantity of metal contained in each would reduce the probability of any attempt at repairs, even were this practicable. The few early examples, consequently, which we are able to present, dating from the fourteenth and fifteenth centuries, are made of bronze or laton, a form of brass, and though not properly coming within our subject, are given as types of the shapes which were no doubt adopted also by the pewterers. Of fourteenth-century make are Nos. 1 and 2 [Plate XII.] in laton and 3 in bronze; and of the fifteenth, 4 and 5 in laton and 6, 7 and 8

NOTES ON THE ILLUSTRATIONS

in bronze. There are, on the other hand, no bronze or laton spoons of sixteenth-century make in this collection, all the twenty-four of that period being pewter. The bowl in each is of the broadly oval shape, characteristic also of earlier examples, which differs so conspicuously from our present spoons in being broadest at the end and narrowing upwards towards the handle—obovate, to employ a botanical term—instead of tapering down from below the handle towards the point. The handles, however, present a considerable variety. Most of them belong to what is known as the " Slip-top " pattern, in which the stem, which has straight parallel sides and is as a rule only slightly flattened, is abruptly and obliquely truncated, presenting an acute angle at one edge, and an obtuse one at the other, as if it had been cut off by a slanting blow from a chisel. Such are Nos. 1, 2, 3, 5, 6 and 7 in Plate XIII., all in Plate XV., and Nos. 1 to 4 and 6 and 9 in Plate XVI. Of these, No. 6 Plate XIII., and Nos. 1, 2, 3 and 6 in Plate XV. all have the same maker's mark with pellets above and below in a dotted circle, and the owner's initial, A, and were all obtained from the same excavation in York Road, Westminster. The remaining four are all different ; one, No. 6 in Plate XIV., is a very curious Sacramental spoon with a half-length figure on a rough capital at the top of the stem, from which it and others of the same form obtain the name of " Maidenhead" spoons ; a second, No. 5 in the same plate, has a roughly moulded hexagonal head with a flat top, hence called " Seal-headed " ; the third, No. 8, also in Plate XIV., is of the familiar " Apostle " design ; while the fourth, No. 1, Plate XIV. again, has an acorn head. The laton spoons again preponderate among those of the seventeenth century, there being no less than twenty-eight, of which only those presenting some marked peculiarity or forms not found in the pewter specimens need be mentioned. No. 4 Plate XIV. is a laton "Apostle" spoon, No. 8 Plate XVII., No. 3 Plate XIV., Nos. 1, 2, 3, 4, 5, 6 and 7, all in Plate XVII., while No. 8 in Plate XX. has a sort of shallow urn-shaped top which is quite peculiar. An equally unusual type is No. 7 Plate XX., which has a very deep circular bowl and a short flattened handle; while in the large gravy spoon, No. 2, we have in both the bowl and the so-called " dog-nose " handle

PLATE CI

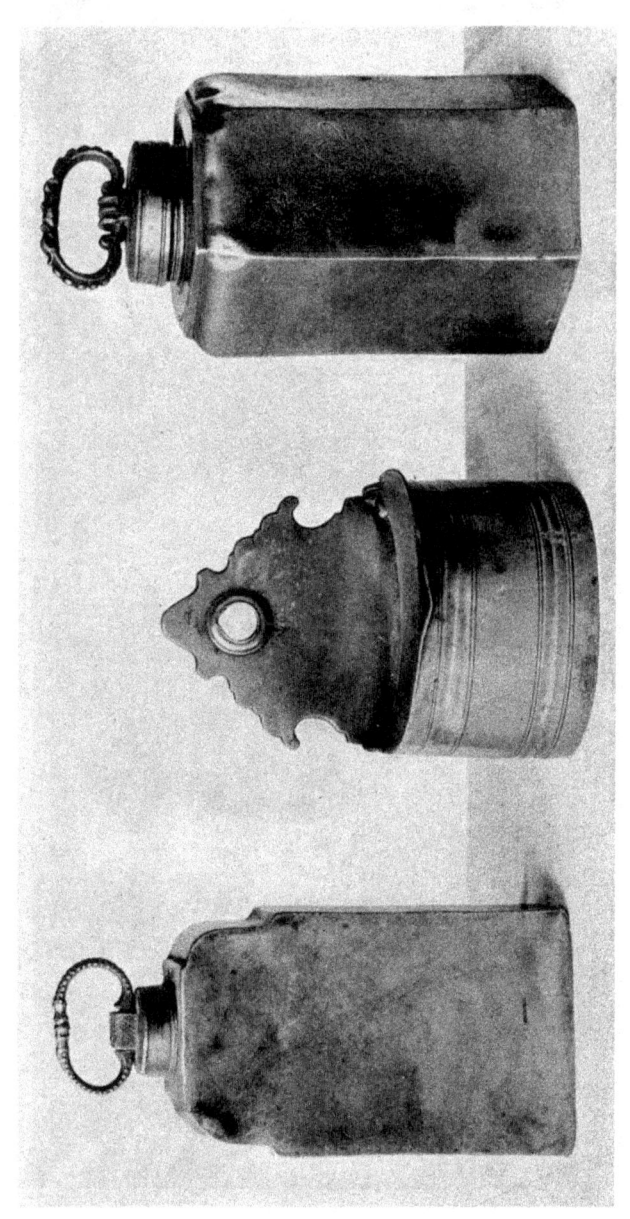

H 12⅜"
FOOD-BOTTLE.

2 H. 9⅛"
SALT-BOX.

3 H. 13"
FOOD-BOTTLE.

PLATE CII

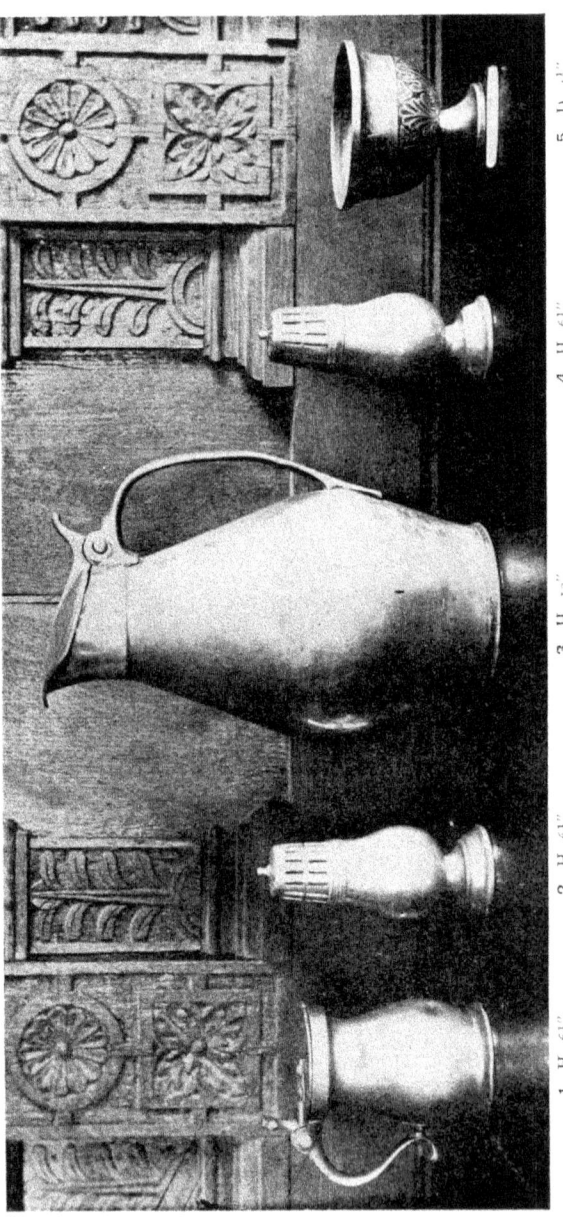

1 H. 6½"   2 H. 6¼"   3 H. 13"   4 H. 6¼"   5 D. 4½"
SHAVING-POT,   SUGAR-SPRINKLER,   CIDER-JUG,   SUGAR-SPRINKLER,   SUGAR-BASIN.
English.   Belgian.   Norman.   Belgian.   Belgian.

NOTES ON THE ILLUSTRATIONS

a distinct tendency towards more modern shapes, and in No. 4, both in the same plate, a curious pierced ladle. Of the pewter spoons, No. 2 Plate XIV., with the seated lion on the handle, is noteworthy. No. 2 Plate XVIII. has a decidedly broadened and flattened sliptop handle of the type known as "Puritan," of which other examples in laton are Nos. 1, 3, 4 and 5, all in the same plate, the notches on the head of the last perhaps indicating the first beginnings of the three-lobed broadened top known as "Pied-de-biche," a further approach to which is seen in No. 6 in the same plate. The subsequent developments of this idea were very varied, and are well illustrated in Plates XVIII. and XIX. Thus in No. 7 Plate XIX. a slight deepening of the notches gives three regularly rounded lobes, a more marked deepening in No. 9 Plate XIX. (a highly ornamented pewter spoon) and No. 8 Plate XVIII. gives a broad round central lobe with a claw-shaped projection on each side. In No. 3 Plate XIX. these are cut off, leaving a single lobe. In No. 4 Plate XIX. the notches are shallow, forming a pear-shaped expansion, and in Nos. 2, 5, and 6 Plate XIX. they are variously modified. Nos. 1

OLD PEWTER

and 3 Plate XX. are eighteenth-century work, evidently founded on the contemporary silver work, and differ little from those made at the present day. The spoons in Plate XI. are of the nineteenth-century make, the soup ladle on the right bearing the initials W. R. flanking a crown and the name ASH BER RY in three separate stamps, while that on the left, the three table-spoons and the ten toddy ladles, are marked JO HN YA TES similarly divided into four, and a crowned V.R.

CHURCH VESSELS

The earliest examples of these, and indeed the most ancient objects here reproduced, are the three Roman vessels from Appleshaw in Plate III., but as these have been fully discussed in an earlier chapter no further reference to them need be made here. The next in point of age is the hexagonal pyx on the left of Plate XXI., with the Annunciation and the Arms of England and France on the lid, which dates from the fourteenth century, while the two patens from a church in Yorkshire on the right of Plate XXII. 3, are of fifteenth-century make. To the seventeenth belong the fine English Communion flagon

NOTES ON THE ILLUSTRATIONS

on the left of the same plate (1), that in the centre of Plate XXI. 2 which bears the date 1677 and came from Midhurst in Sussex, and probably the Dutch earthenware flagon mounted in pewter in the centre of Plate XXV. 2. The two other flagons in Plates XXIV. 3 and XXIII., one with, the other without, a spout, though belonging to the earlier flat-lidded type, are eighteenth-century work, and to the same period may be attributed the various forms of chalice, those in Plates XXIV. 2, XXVI. 1 and 3, and XXVII. being English, that on the left of Plate XXV. 3, and those in Plates XXVIII. 2 and XXIX. 1, Scotch, the latter dated 1804, while that on the right of Plate XXV. 1 is Italian. An uncommon object is the minute pocket Communion set in Plate XXX. 1, the chalice in which is only two inches high, with its roughly carved wooden case, which comes from Iceland. Rare also are the two Communion cruets, or chapnets, in Plate XXX. 2, 4, of French or Flemish workmanship, their respective uses being indicated by the letter which forms the handle to the lid, A on the left for *Aqua*, V. on the right for *Vinum*, of which last a second and more graceful specimen stands on the extreme left of Plate XXXI. 1. The portable bénitiers, so often mentioned in mediæval wills and inventories, are well represented, that in Plate V. being adapted for suspending only, 2, 3 and 4 in Plate VI. for either hanging or standing, while 1 in the same plate could only be used on a table or altar. They are all of Flemish make, as are the church candlesticks in Plates XXXII. 1 and 3, and XXXIII., and the candelabrum in Plate XXXIV.

DOMESTIC CANDLESTICKS AND LAMPS.

Candlesticks, being easily made strong and not necessarily subject to much handling, are comparatively common, and do not as a rule present any marked differences from those of the same dates made in brass or silver. Those in the centre and on the left of Plate XXXVI. 1 and 2 are Scotch, the pair on the right of the same plate (3) Dutch. The larger one in Plate XXXVII. 3 is French, and the little taper-holder on the left of it (2) Flemish. Lamps are more rarely found in good condition, and the three of German eighteenth-century make in Plate XXXVII. 1, 4 and 5 are exceptionally interesting,

PLATE CIII

1 H. 4″ D. 2¾″
MUG. William IV.

2 H. 9½″ D. 5½″
FLAGON. XVIII century.

3 H. 6½″ D. 4½″
TANKARD. Late XVIII century.

4 H. 3″ D. 2¼″
MUG. Early XIX century.

PLATE CIV

PLATE XII 1 | 2 | 5 | 5 | 2

PLATE XIII 1 | 3 | 5 | 5 | 7

PLATE XIV 1 | 4 | 6 | 7 | 6 | 8

NOTES ON THE ILLUSTRATIONS

though still more so are those with glass reservoirs in Plate XXXVIII. In these the metal band which supports the oil-holder is divided into numbered spaces, by means of which, as the lamp burned and the oil sank down, the passage of the night hours was roughly indicated. That this would be fairly accurate in the flat and cylindrical forms (1, 3 and 5) is easy to believe, but the later hours in the two with pear-shaped reservoirs (2 and 4) must have appeared to have sped much more rapidly than the earlier ones, since, at any rate, no alteration has been made in the distances apart of the divisions to compensate for the reduced bulk of oil contained between each two.

CUPS AND TANKARDS

The line of demarkation between these two and between the second and flagons is not always an easy one to draw, but, speaking broadly, the first may be defined as drinking-vessels with two handles or none, the second as one-handled vessels intended to be drunk out of, and the last as similar vessels destined to hold liquors which were poured into others for the consumer. Cups may be conveniently divided into two classes, those with stems, and those without. The former, with the exception of a certain type to be considered hereafter, are rarely met with in pewter, and when they do occur are generally those direct imitations of silver-work which have perhaps been more than sufficiently deprecated already, and there is consequently no necessity for pointing out the constructional defects in the four cups, light and graceful as they are in design, represented in Plate XLI. The stemmed cups, mostly made in Germany for the use of various trade guilds, are less uncommon, and examples are to be found in most large collections. Like much other German work, they are apt to show a tendency to exaggeration of outline and over-redundancy of ornament, but the simpler forms, such as those shown in Plates XXXII. 2 and XLII. 1 and 3, are not without a certain dignity. A beautiful example of the stemless type is the little English cup on the left of Plate XXVIII. 1. The "beaker" or "tumbler" shape, illustrated in Plates XLIII. 2 and XLIV. 4, is far commoner, these having been largely imported from the Netherlands into Scotland, where, after the Reformation, they

NOTES ON THE ILLUSTRATIONS

seem to have been generally used as Communion cups.

Tankards, again, may be considered as falling into two categories, those with lids and those without. The most usual form of the first is that with straight sides more or less relieved by hoops and bands, as in the one on the right of Plate IX. 3, the four in Plate XLVI., and one in the centre of Plate XLV. 2, or slightly conical or curved, as in Plates XLIII. 1 and 3, and XLVIII. 3, but from these simple lines we find every graduation to the full, bold curves of the "balustrade" type, illustrated in the middle of Plate L. 3, or such fantastic designs as the German guild tankard, dated 1645, on the right of Plate XLIX. 3. Simplicity, as a rule, marks the lidless tankard, characteristic examples of which are shown in Plates XLIV. 1, XCIII. 2, and CIII. 3.

OLD PEWTER

MEASURES

The segregation of these is often, it must be owned, somewhat arbitrary, since they graduate indefinitely into tankards on the one hand and flagons on the other, for measures such as the Scotch half-mutchkin, gill, half-gill, and half-glass [Plates XXXI. 3, 2, 6, 5, and 4, LV. and LVI.], and the English one which stands second from the right hand in Plate XLIV. 3, were undoubtedly used as drinking-vessels, while the flagon-shaped one on the left of it (2), and those in Plates IX. 1, LVII. 2 and 3, and LVIII. 4, are equally well adapted for filling round. Most interesting among these last are the Tappit-hens previously mentioned, examples of which are given in Plates VIII. 2, LXI. and LX., the last in especial being of unusual importance. Mr. Ingleby Wood could only rely upon tradition for the fact that hot drinks were brought out in these vessels to the passengers upon coaches at the changing-places, and served round in a small pewter cup, but we have direct proof in the existence still in its place of the cup fitting into the throat of the vessel.

PLATE CV

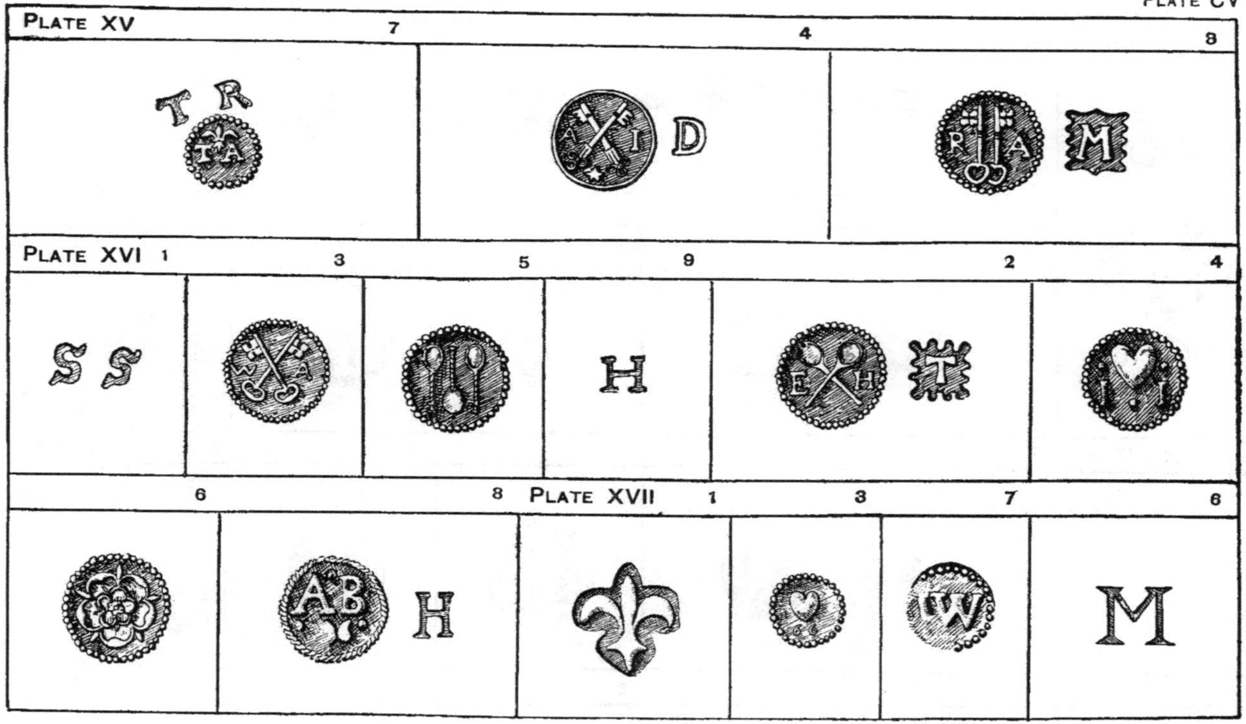

| PLATE XV | | | | PLATE XVI | | | | | PLATE XVII | | | | |

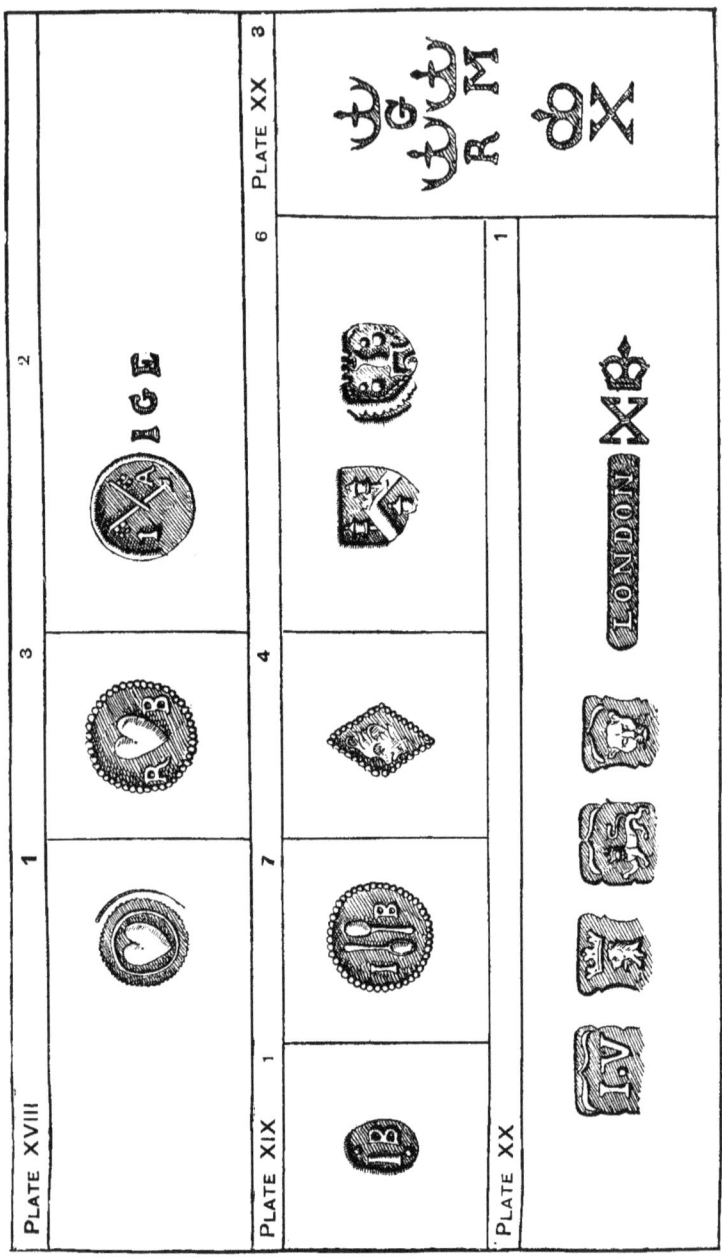

NOTES ON THE ILLUSTRATIONS

FLAGONS AND JUGS

There is probably more diversity of shape and size in these than in any other class of vessels, and many of them are remarkable for their unforced beauty of line and proportion. It would be hard, for instance, to improve upon those reproduced in Plates LVIII. 2 and LXII., both of which are English, the former eighteenth, the latter seventeenth century. The German taste was, as usual, more ornate, but there is much dignity in the large guild flagons in Plates LI., LIII., LXIII. 3, and XLII. 2.

PORRINGERS

These, which are frequently, and generally erroneously, called bleeding-bowls or barber's bowls, were very commonly in use in the Middle Ages, and great numbers of them still exist. The ornamentation of the bowl when present was generally confined to a Tudor rose in relief on the bottom, as in Plates LXIX. 2 and LVII. 1, but a considerable freedom of treatment was allowed in the handles. In some cases these were quite plain, or with a slightly curved outline [Plate

OLD PEWTER

LXX]. In the one on the left of Plate LXIX. 1 the border is deeply crenated, in that on the right of the same plate and in those in Plates LVII. 1 and LXXI. 1 and 3 the ears are elegantly and elaborately pierced, while in Plate XXVIII. 3 we have a rare instance of solid ears with a pattern in relief.

PLATES AND DISHES

Beyond doubt these are the commonest objects which will come under the collector's notice, ranging in point of date from the Appleshaw Roman pewter [Plates I. and II.] up to the present day, and in size from a few inches in diameter to two feet or more [Plate LXV. 2 and 3]. The rims of the plates were originally quite plain, or strengthened by a plain band below. This in later days was placed above, and frequently adorned with mouldings, as in Plates XXII. 2, LVIII. 4, LXV. 2, and LXXIII. 3, while in the eighteenth century the rim was often broken into curves and the border variously beaded or moulded in imitation of silver work [Plates IX. 2, and LXXIII. 1 and 5]. The surface also presented temptations to

NOTES ON THE ILLUSTRATIONS

the would-be decorator, as shown in Plates XXXV. and XLV. 1.

TABLE PLATE

Practically every article used in the serving or consuming of food has been at one time or another manufactured in pewter. We have soup-tureens [Plate LXXV.], vegetable dishes [Plates LXV. 1 and 4, and LXXVI. 1], ewers and basins for washing the hands [Plate LXXVII.] and bowls for washing the dishes [Plate LXXVIII.]. Salt cellars, pepper and mustard pots appear in a variety of forms too large to specify in detail [Plates LXXX. to LXXXIV. and others], but note must be made of a curious kind of vinegar sprinkler of Scottish origin which exactly resembles in its construction the small spirit lamps often handed to-day to after-dinner smokers [Plates LXXXIII. 4 and LXXXV. 6]. When tea came into general use pewter was devoted to its service. The herb was kept in pewter bottles [Plate LXXXVI. 2 and 4], and urns [Plate LXXXVII.], tea and coffee pots, milk jugs, and sugar bowls [Plates LXXXVIII. &c.] replaced the earlier beer jug and tankard at the breakfast table.

OLD PEWTER

Even the matutinal egg appeared in a pewter cup [Plate XCI.], and the whole was sometimes brought in on a pewter tray [Plate LXXVI. 2].

MISCELLANEOUS OBJECTS

The number and variety of these is almost infinite. Boxes to hold tobacco [Plates LXXIV. 6, XCIV. 3, and XCV. 3] and snuff [Plates XCVI. 1 and 3, and XCVII. 4] for the master, spices [Plate XXIX. 2], powder or patches [Plate LXXXVI. 3], sugar [Plate XC. 2] or other trifles for the mistress [Plates XL. 3, and XC. 2], inkpots of diverse sorts [Plates XCV. 2, XCVIII. 1 and 2, and XCIX. 2], shoe buckles [Plate XCVI. 2 and 4, and buttons [Plate V. 3] were only a tithe of the fancy articles turned out by the trifler. In the East pewter was even allowed the honour of adorning weapons [Plate C.].

A puzzle which few people succeed in solving unaided is presented by the object in the centre of Plate LVIII. 3. It is a round vessel pierced with holes and closed by a screw lid with a twisted handle, and was, and doubtless still is, used by the French peasant women to keep the rice apart from

NOTES ON THE ILLUSTRATIONS

the meat and broth with which it was boiled. Another puzzle which still awaits solution is the exact purpose to which the screw-top bottles in Plate CI. 1 and 3 were devoted. They are generally six-sided, though the one on the left of our plate is flattened, and in the catalogue of the Clifford's Inn Exhibition are called food-bottles or food carriers, but this title seems to be merely speculative, and there is yet opportunity for some pewter-lover to tell us what they really were.

USEFUL BOOKS OF REFERENCE

History of the Worshipful Company of Pewterers of the City of London. Based upon their own Records. By CHARLES WELCH, F.S.A. Two vols., 4to. (1902.)

Pewter Plate. A Historical and Descriptive Handbook. By H. J. L. MASSÉ, M.A. (1904.)

Scottish Pewter-Ware and Pewterers. By L. INGLEBY WOOD. (1905.)

Les Métaux dans l'antiquité et au moyen age. L'Etain. Par GERMAIN BAPST. Avec 11 planches, &c. Paris. (1884.)

Old Scottish Communion Plate. By THOMAS BURNS. F.R.S.E. With a Preface by the Right Rev. J. MACGREGOR ... and Chronological Tables of Scottish Hall-marks, prepared by A. J. S. BROOK. Illustrated. (1892.)

Dictionnaire de l'Ameublement et de la Décoration depuis le xiiie siècle jusqu'a nos jours. Par HENRI HAVARD. Four vols., 4to. Paris. (1887-90.)

Histoire du Mobilier : recherches et notes sur les objets d'art qui peuvent composer l'ameublements et les collections de l'homme du monde et du curieux. Par ALBERT JACQUEMART. 8vo. Paris. (1876.)

François Briot, Caspar Enderlein und das Edelzinn. VON HANS DEMIANI. 4to. Leipzig. (1897.).

The Perth Hammermen Book. With an Introductory Sketch by COLIN A. HUNT of Perth. 4to. (1889.)

The Church Plate of the County of Northampton. By C. A. MARKHAM. Illustrated. 8vo. (1894.)

The Church Plate of the County of Dorset. With Extracts from the Returns of Church Goods by the Dorset Commissioners of Edward VI. By the Rev. JAMES E. NIGHTINGALE. (1889.)

The Church Plate of the County of Wilts. Including that part of the County now in the Diocese of Gloucester and Bristol. From Returns made by the Rev. J. E. NIGHTINGALE and the Rev. E. H. GODDARD. (1891.)

The Church Plate of the County of Norfolk. By the Rev. J. E. NIGHTINGALE.

An Inventory of the Church Plate of Leicestershire, with some Account of the Donors. With Plates. By ANDREW TROLLOPE. (1890.)

Elizabethan England. From a Description of England by William Harrison in " Hollinshed's Chronicles." Edited by LOTHROP WITHINGTON. With an Introduction by F. J. FURNIVALL. "Camelot Classics" (1886.)

INDEX

ABERNETHIE, WILLIAM, of Edinburgh, fined 1652, for using bad metal, 103
" Acorn-head ' pattern. See Spoons
Allen, Thomas, forbidden to assist a new invention, 103
Alloy:
Proportions variable, 8; proportions in Roman and English pewter, 8–11; proportions legalised, 11–14; proportions in 1350, 13; object of regulations, 14; inconsistencies in analysis, 15; discussed at the Society of Arts, *ib.*; proportions not of practical importance to the collector, 17; simple method of analysis, 18–23; precautions taken in assaying the metal of the worker, 29; purchase by night forbidden, 32; alloy resembling gold made by a Nuremberg craftsman, 82
Alms Dish. See Church Vessels, &c.
Amadel, Robert, reference, 91
Altar Candlesticks. See Church Vessels, &c.
Anglo-Saxon work, specimens in the Guildhall Museum, London, 52
Antimony, its proportions in some kinds of pewter, 11; separation by analysis only possible to a trained chemist, 23; references, 12, 28, 32
Apostle spoons. See Spoons
Appleshaw, discovery of Roman specimens at, 45, 52, 160. See *plates* I, II, III

Apprenticeship, the "essay" and subsequent registration of private "touch," 26, 27
Aquæ Neriæ, analysis of fourth-century specimens found at, 10
" Archæologia," inventory of the contents of a house at Gillingham, quoted, 87; references, 9, 46
Arnold, Henrici, of Ilsington, a donor of Church pewter, 1641, 100
Arthur Tudor, reference, 90
" Arts, Journal of the Society of," discussion on alloys, quoted, 8, 15
Ashberry, his mark, *plate* XI, iv; 14, 52
Ath, reference, 57
Augsburg, reference, 57
Avesne, Jeanne d', a French craftsman, 1516, 74

BAPST, M. Germain, on Roman alloy, 10; references, 63, 71, 134
Barber's Bowl. See Bowls
Barry, Mrs. F. W., rose-water dish in her possession provided for Charles I., 102
Battersea, composition of Roman metal found at, 11
Beaker. See Bowls
Beer-Jugs:
English; eighteenth century; *plate* LXVI, iii, 94
Students' Beer-Jug; German; seventeenth century; *plate* LXXIII, ii, 104
Belgian Pewter: Bruges craftsmen noted for porringers and flasks, 55; the guild at Ath in

OLD PEWTER

Belgian Pewter—*cont.*
1328, 57 ; Mons a centre in 1353, 58 ; craft well supported at Ghent, *ib.* ; Bruges craftsmen support the town militia, 1376, 59 ; Mons marks in 1467, 67
Bénitier. See Church Vessels, &c.
Bermondsey, spoons found at, See *plates* XIII, i, 18 ; XIV, vii, 20 ; XV, viii, 21 ; XVI, i, iii, iv, v, vi, 22 ; XVIII, ii, 26 ; XIX, iv, v, 28 ; XX, iii, 29
Boileau, Etienne, his account of the Paris guilds in thirteenth century, alluded to, 55
Boissonet, l'Abbé, his method of "scouring" quoted by M. Bapst, reference, 134
Bourbon, the Duke de, his pewter vessels, 1507, 73
Bowls :
    Barber's Bowl, English ; eighteenth century ; *plate* LXIX, i ; 100, 160
    Beaker, engraved ; early eighteenth century ; mark, a crowned rose ; *plate* XLIV, iv ; 64, 156
    Beaker, Scotch ; eighteenth century ; *plate* XLIII, ii ; 62, 156
    Bowls ; *plate* LXV, i, iv ; 103, 161
    Bowl ; marks, crowned rose and W.R.W. ; *plate* LXXI, iii ; 101, 160
    Bowl, Flemish ; seventeenth century ; *plate* LXXVIII, i ; 112, 161
    Bowl, Scotch ; mark on one lug indecipherable ; *plate* LXXI, i ; 101, 160
    Two-handed bowl ; *plate* LVIII, i ; 82
    —— Dutch ; eighteenth century ; *plate* LXIX, ii ; 100, 159

Box, Edward, London, disregards advertising rule, 115
Box ; no mark ; *plate* LXXXVI, iii ; 118, 162
Briot, François, references, 3, 42, 79, 95, 137
Britannia metal, &c., aids the downfall of pewter, 117
British Museum, Decorated specimens at, 80 ; references, 45, 48 ; see also *plates* I, II, III
Brown-Austen, Professor, reference, 15
Brown, George, Perth tinsmith, applies for relief, 114
Bruges, references, 32, 55, 59
Bryan, Mr. H., specimen in his possession made by the Master of the Company, 123
Burgundy, Duke of, establishes Guilds, 1478, 68 ; his pewter more decorative, 1507, 73
Burns, Robert, reference, 139
Burton, spoon-maker, 1686, unwillingly allowed to use a lathe, 36
Buschius of Hildesheim, his record of Saxon pewter, 1470, 68
Buttons, Two ; *plate* V, iii ; 10, 162

CAMPBELL, PATRICK, reference, 113
Candelabrum, Flemish ; eighteenth century ; *plate* XXXIV ; 52, 154
Candlesticks :
    Candlestick, French ; eighteenth century ; *plate* XXIX, iii ; 44, 154
    —— French ; *plate* XXXVII. iii ; 56, 154
    Candlesticks ; *plates* XXXIX, i, ii, iii ; 60, 154
    —— eighteenth century; *plates* XL, i, iv ; 60, 154
    —— Dutch ; eighteenth century ; *plate* XXXVI, iii ; 54, 154

INDEX

Candlesticks—*cont.*
—— Scotch ; eighteenth century ; *plate* XXXVI, i ; 54, 154
—— Scotch ; nineteenth century ; no marks ; *plate* XXXVI, ii ; 54, 154
Taper-Holder, Flemish ; *plate* XXXVII, ii ; 56, 154
Gloucester Candlestick, The, twelfth century ; *plate* IV ; 5, 54
Canterbury, Richard, Archbishop of, reference, 53
Capdeville, Pierre de, of Bordeaux, extracts from inventory, 1591, 88
"Cardinal's hatte" mould, 35
Carel, a Nuremberg pewterer, 1324, 57
Casket, French ; sixteenth century ; *plate* LXXI, ii ; 101
Cassiterides, the "Tin Islands" mentioned by Herodotus, 31
Catherine of Arragon, reference 90
Cavendish, his account of Wolsey's plate, 91
Chabrolles, Mark Henry, a Frenchman, refused permission to trade in London, 1688, 106
Chalice. See Church Vessels
"Chapnets." See Church Vessels, &c.
Charles II., references, 104, 108
Charles V., reference, 69
Charles VI., reference, 60
Charles VII. of France, his extensive purchase in 1422, 64
Charterhous, John, refuses to restore two candlesticks at Edinburgh, 1559, 81, 82
Chichely, Robert, Lord Mayor of London, ordains the use of pewter by ale-dealers, 1423, 64
Chinese, conjecture as to the invention of pewter by the, 44

Chopin, a Scottish measure, 61, 132
Church Flagon. See Church Vessels, &c.
Church Vessels, &c. :
Alms Dish ; Scotch ; eighteenth century ; marked AS. IK ; *plate* XXII, ii ; 32, 160
—— English ; eighteenth century ; *plate* XXIV, i ; 36
—— German ; early eighteenth century ; *plate* XXXV, 53, 161
Altar Candlesticks ; eighteenth century ; *plate* XXXII, i, iii ; 48, 154
—— Flemish ; seventeenth century ; *plate* XXXIII, i, ii ; 50, 154
Bénitier, probably Flemish ; no marks ; *plate* V ; 6, 57, 154
Bénitiers, Flemish ; eighteenth century ; *plate* VI, i, ii, iii, iv ; 8, 57, 154
Chalice and Paten, from Kriswick ; *plate* XXI, iii ; 30
Chalice, Italian ; no marks ; *plate* XXV, i ; 34, 153
—— Scotch ; no marks ; *plate* XXV, iii ; 34, 153
—— English ; eighteenth century ; *plate* XXIV, ii ; 36, 153
Chalices and Church Flagon ; English ; *plate* XXVI, i, ii, iii ; 38, 153
Chalices, English ; eighteenth century ; *plate* XXVII, i, ii, iii ; 40, 153
"Chapnets," small church vessels, 95, 153
Church Flagon, Scotch ; early eighteenth century type ; *plate* XXIII ; 37, 153
Communion Cup ; Scotch ; *plate* XXVIII, ii ; 42
—— 1804 ; *plate* XXIX, i ; 44, 153

167

Church Vessels, &c.—*cont.*
Communion Flagon ; English ; from Midhurst Church, Sussex ; frontispiece ; *plate* XXI, ii ; 30, 153
—— Flagon ; English ; seventeenth century ; *plate* XXII, i ; 32, 153
—— Jug, earthenware, mounted in pewter ; mark : angel standing holding crossed branch ; letters indistinct ; *plate* XXV, ii ; 34, 153
Laver, Scotch ; late eighteenth century ; *plate* XXIV, iii ; 36 153
Patens, from a Church in Yorkshire, England ; fifteenth century ; *plate* XXII, iii ; 32, 152
Pocket Communion Service, in wooden case, bought in Iceland, probably Danish or Scotch ; *plate* XXX, i ; 45, 153
Pyx, hexagonal ; English ; fourteenth century ; *plate* XXI, i ; 30, 152
Sacramental Cruet ; Aqua ; French or Flemish ; *plate* XXX, ii ; 45, 153
—— Cruet ; Vinum ; French or Flemish ; *plate* XXX, iv ; 45, 153
—— Spoon, with " Maidenhead " top, found in London ; sixteenth century ; *plate* XIV, vi ; 20, 150
Church, utilisation of pewter for the ; early records, 52 ; its use forbidden, 1175, 53 ; its exclusion found impracticable in France, 54 ; vessels in use at St. Stephen's, Coleman Street, London, 1467, 67 ; vessels at the Cistercian Convent of St. Martin, 68 ; at

Church—*cont.*
the Convent of St. Cyr, *ib.* ; very little recorded at the dissolution of the monasteries, 76 ; Chrismatory and pyx bought, 1554, by Waltham Abbey, 80 ; the plate of St. Giles, Edinburgh, removed for safety, 1559, 81 ; disappearance of much pre-Reformation plate in Scotland in 1559, 82 ; destruction of church plate during the sixteenth century, 92 ; purchase at Strood, 1607, 94 ; safe to assume that no pewter Church flagons are earlier than 1603, 94 ; inscription on vessel at Werrington, 95 ; effects of the revolution of 1617 in the Church of Scotland, 97 ; first appearance of the " laver," *ib.* ; earliest examples, 152 ; English, Scotch, Italian, Icelandic, and French or Flemish specimens, 153
Cider Jug, Norman ; *plate* CII, iii ; 140
Clifford's Inn Exhibition, references, 127, 147, 163
Cœur, Jacques, supplies pewter for his work-people, 66
Coffee Pots :
Eighteenth century ; *plate* LXXXVIII, iii ; 122, 161
Dutch ; no marks ; *plate* LXVII, ii ; 96
Flemish ; eighteenth century ; *plate* XCV, i ; 132
French ; eighteenth century ; *plate* LXXXIX, ii ; 124
Louis XIV. style ; German ; first half of eighteenth century ; *plate* XC, i ; 125
Collecting : not a fashionable craze, 1 ; its attractions as compared with other objects, 2 ; taste increasing, 4 ; examination of good specimens

INDEX

Collecting—*cont.*
essential, *ib.*; aim and scope of the book, 5; proportions of alloy not important, 17; pewter Church flagons before 1603 unlikely, 94; collecting and displaying, 120; difficulties caused by imperfect records of the companies, *ib.*; five plates of "touches" at Pewterers' Hall, 121; paucity of marks on existing specimens, *ib.*; confusing effects of early rules, 122; Edinburgh "touches" more instructive than those of London, 124; advice to owners of vessels with private "touches," 125; marks generally misleading and confusing, 125; Nuremberg almost the only marks not duplicated elsewhere, 127; reasons for the absence of marks, 128; effects of the use of old moulds by travelling pewterers, 130; style, practically, the only indication of time and place of manufacture, *ib.*; differences between Scotch and English measures, 132; knowledge of contemporary work of gold- and silver-smiths valuable, 133; Boissonet's rules for "scouring," 134; coats of arms doubtful indications of date, 134; experience and genuine interest in the subject necessary, 135; some of the articles collectors may hope to find, 136; unadvisable to render old pewter indistinguishable from new, 145
Communion Cups, &c. See Church Vessels, &c.
Cornwall, its metals, 30, 32
Cream Jugs:
Plate LXIV, iii, 92; *plate* LXXXVI, v, 118

Cream Jugs—*cont.*
English; eighteenth century; *plate* L, i, v; 74
Early nineteenth century; *plate* LXXXVIII, ii; 122, 161
Scotch; *plate* LXXXII, i; 116
Scotch; no mark; *plate* LXXXVI, i; 118
Cromwell, Oliver, reference, 103
"Crooked Lane men" and their ware in 1634, 98; references, 99, 105
"Crooked Lane men" and their ware in 1634, 98
Cruets:
Cruet, Vinum; no marks; *plate* XXXI, i; 46, 154
Cruet-Stand; German; Middle of eighteenth century; *plate* XLIX, ii; 72
Cruets, Set of; Scotch; eighteenth century; *plate* LXXXV iii, iv, v; 118
Cumberland, Duke of, reference, 114
Cups. See Tankards

Dagger, Oriental; pewter and bone; sheath bound with pewter: *plate* C, 136, 162
Danby, John, of Alveston, his pewter of 1444, 66
Decoration: characteristics of good specimens, 40; supposed embellishments probably not the work of the maker, 41; chasers alluded to by Jean de Jeandun, 1323, 56; François Briot famous in sixteenth century, 79; gilding and painting prohibited, 1564, 82; development of French and German decorated ware during the sixteenth century, 92
Dishes:
English; seventeenth century; *plate* XLV, i; 68, 161

Dishes—*cont.*
English; eighteenth century (?); date 1689; *plate* LXV, ii; 103, 160
—— middle of eighteenth century; *plate* IX, ii; 12, 111, 160
—— eighteenth century; *plate* LXXIII, iii; 104, 160
—— Scotch; sixteenth century; *plate* LXXIV, ii; 106
—— sixteenth century; *plate* XLV, iii; 68
Roman; found at Appleshaw; *plates* I, II, III; 1, 2, 4, 47, 48, 49, 160
Displaying: original surroundings the best, 137; its utility to be considered in the choice of surroundings, *ib.*; its homeliness appeals to the sympathetic and imaginative, 138; its limitations and individuality, 139; incongruous proximity to choicer objects to be avoided, 140; suggestions for housing and placing, 141; cleaning and repairing, 142; evidences of age to be preserved, 145
" Dog-nose " handle. See Spoons
Dyer, Lawrence, fined for working a new invention, 103

EDWARD I., pewter used at his coronation, 54; confirms charter to the Stanners, 56
Edward IV. confers a charter on the Guild, 1473, 68
Egg-Cups:
English; eighteenth century; *plate* L, iv; 74
—— with bead pattern; eighteenth century; *plate* XCVII, v; 133
Scotch; set of six; no marks; *plate* XCI, iv–ix; 126, 162
No marks; *plate* XCI, i, ii, iii; 126, 162

Ely, John, Vicar of Ripon, his bequest, 1427, 65
Enderlein, Gaspard, references, 3, 42, 95, 137
Engleheart, Rev. C. H., dishes found at Appleshaw by, *plates* I, II, III, 1, 2, 4; his deductions concerning the marks on, 47, 48; references, 45, 46, 49
English Pewter: moulds owned in common, 33; foreign importations prohibited, 38; some causes of decadence, 42; its domestic use first mentioned in 1274, 54; the craft established in London in 1347, 57; master and wardens appointed to enforce ordinances, 1348, 58; during fourteenth century used principally by the Court, nobility, and Church dignitaries, 62; outcry in the fourteenth century against pedlars and unlicensed workmen, 62; York, in 1419, the principal trading place for the North of England, 64; its use ordained, in 1423, by retailers of ale, 64; bequest by John Ely, Vicar of Ripon, 65; London pewterers prosperous in 1438, 66; pewter possessed by John Danby in 1444, 66; its use by the nobility declining in 1459, 66; partly religious nature of the London Guild, 67; importations from England stamped by the importers in 1467, with a crowned rose, 67; pewter bought in 1470, by the Goldsmiths' Company, *ib.*; Edward IV. confers a charter on the Guild, 68; Lady Uvedale's bequest in 1487, 69; stamp and seal of London Guild, 1492, 69; development during fifteenth century tends to-

INDEX

English Pewter—*cont.*
wards articles of domestic use, 71; at beginning of sixteenth century too expensive to be common, 72; in 1503 marks and "touches" made compulsory, *ib.*; Guilds, in 1504, restricted in their powers with regard to disputes, 73; craft complains of "strangers" and false weights, 1512, 74; troubled by foreign competition, 1535, 75; protective measures passed in 1538, 76; special marks ordained for York craftsmen, 1540, 77; stamping pewter lids for stoneware vessels compulsory, 80; buying at night by pewterers prohibited, 32, 80; number of apprentices limited, 82; pewter in great demand in middle of sixteenth century, 83; London Company privileged to charge royalties on smelting and casting of tin, 90; pewter falls into disuse by the higher classes, 90; provincial competition, 93; increased activity in 1612, 95; distinctions between various branches of craftsmen relaxed, 96; new uses in 1614, 97; Lord Northampton's pewter in 1614, *ib.*; the pewter of Sir Thomas Hoskyns in 1615, *ib.*; clamour for the suppression of "deceivable hawkers" in 1621, 98; pewterers imitate the marks of the Goldsmiths' Company, 1635, 99; 1641 the earliest date of Dorsetshire pewter, 100; restrictive methods of the London Company, 103; pewter cisterns and toys appear in 1667, 105; penalty for making inferior toys, *ib.*; exclusion of a French craftsman, 106; in-

English Pewter—*cont.*
consistent attitude of the London Company in 1690, 107; decline of the craft evident at end of the seventeenth century, *ib.*; craft declines during eighteenth and nineteenth centuries, 109; rule against self-advertisement falls into disuse, 1727, 110; London Company powerless, *ib.*, 113, 115; practical extinction of the craft in the nineteenth century, 117, 118; last "touch" registered at Pewterers' Hall, 1824, *ib.*; efforts to revive the craft inappreciable, 119
Ewer, Robert, sells pewter, 1607, 94
Ewer and Basin; *plate* LXXVII, 111, 161
—— and Cover; German; *plate* XLIX; i, 72

FAIRFAX, Sir William, his "sallite" dishes, 34; inventory of the contents of his house at Gillingham, quoted, 87
Falstolfe, Sir John, reference, 66; "Fasson d'argent," a sign of decadence, 42; vessels made of, 61; reference, 73
"Feast vessels," the loan of, 40
FitzHenry, J. H., Esq., cruet-stand and sugar-box given by; *plates* XLIX, ii, XC, ii; 72, 125
Flagons and Jugs:
Flagon; *plate* LXIV, ii; 92
—— seventeenth century; *plate* XCIX, i; 134
—— seventeenth century; *plate* XCIX, iii; 134
—— Imitation Chinese Dutch; seventeenth century; *plate* LXIII, ii; 90
—— German; seventeenth century; *plate* LXIII; iii., 90, 159

Flagons and Jugs—*cont.*
Flagon ; eighteenth century ; *plate* CIII, ii ; 142
—— 1706, Nuremberg mark ; *plate* XLII, ii ; 62, 159
—— German ; eighteenth century ; *plate* XLIII, i ; 62, 157
—— German ; eighteenth century ; *plate* XLIII, iii ; 62, 157
—— Probably Scotch ; eighteenth century ; *plate* LXIII, i ; 90
Jug ; Dutch ; early eighteenth century ; *plate* LXXVIII, ii ; 112
—— Covered ; Archangel mark ; *plate* LXIV, i ; 92
—— Dutch ; mark, crossed rose ; *plate* LXVII, i ; 96
—— Dutch ; mark, a rose ; *plate* LXVII, iii ; 96
—— English ; seventeenth century ; *plate* LXII, 88, 159
—— English ; eighteenth century ; *plate* XLVIII, ii ; 70
—— English ; eighteenth century ; *plate* LXVI, ii ; 94
—— French ; eighteenth century ; *plate* LXVI, i ; 94
—— George IV. ; *plate* LXVIII ; 98
Fly, Tim, his punning device, 123
Food Bottle ; square ; *plate* CI, i ; 138, 163
—— Bottle ; sexagonal ; *plate* CI, iii ; 138, 163
Forks : pewter forks mentioned in a French inventory of 1672, 105 ; their rarity, 147 ; Fork, small, no mark ; *plate* XI, ii ; 14
François I., reference, 74

French Pewter : proportions of alloy during the eighteenth century, 13 ; mentioned in Boileau's account of the Paris Guilds in the thirteenth century, 55 ; mentioned in a further list of Parisian craftsmen, *ib.* ; Guild prosperous in 1304, *ib.* ; edict against inferior alloys passed at Poitiers, 1333, 57 ; Guild at Rouen, 1369, 58 ; vessels owned by Henri de Poitiers, Bishop of Troyes, 59 ; vessels considered as perquisites by court attendants, 59 ; Michelet the Breton, a craftsman of 1380, 59 ; record in 1380 of a Bénitier in the possession of Jean de Halomesnil, 60 ; store possessed by a canon of Troyes, 1386, 60 ; the reward for workmanship very slight, *ib.* ; the city of Amiens buys pewter from Thibaut la Rue, *ib.* ; the city of Rouen purchases a gallon flagon, 61 ; bequest of the Archbishop of Rheims, 1389, 61 ; Isabel de Moncel, a Parisian craftswoman of 1395, *ib.* ; misapplied use of a wine measure by one Jean Le Bœuf, 1396, *ib.* ; tools used at Rouen, 1402, 63 ; Isabella of Bavaria's order for the Hotel St. Pol, 1401, 63 ; Guillebert of Metz a noted maker, 1407, 64 ; extensive purchase by Charles VII. of France in 1422, 64 ; Jacques Cœur in 1453 supplies pewter for his workpeople, 66 ; Amiens buys pewter cups for noble visitors, 1463, 67 ; Duke of Burgundy in 1478 establishes Guilds, 68 ; pewter bottles in the " Livre des Mestiers " of Charles V., 69 ; increase of

INDEX

French Pewter—*cont.*
craftsmen during the fifteenth century, 71 ; the "silver fashion" increases in favour, 1507, 73 ; Duke of Burgundy's vessels, in 1507, incline to a decorative character, 73 ; Duke of Bourbon's vessels in 1507, *ib*. ; Amiens buys vessel in 1507 from Pierre Hemeron, *ib*. ; in 1516 from Jeanne d'Avesne, 74 ; Paris silversmiths take action against the pewterers, 1545, 79 ; Briot famous as a decorator of pewter, sixteenth century, 79 ; Paris draper's considerable bequest, 1572, 83 ; extracts from inventory of Pierre de Capdeville of Bordeaux, 1591, 88 ; development of decorated ware during sixteenth century, 92 ; decline, except the ornamental kind, during first half of seventeenth century, 102 ; pewter spoons and forks mentioned in French inventory 1672, 105
Galbraith, Glasgow, his mark ; *plate* XLIV, i ; 64, 157
Gardner, Mr. Starkie, quoted, 8, 9, 12, 14
German Pewter : development of the industry, 1324, 57 ; Sebaldus Ruprecht famous for pewter which could be mistaken for silver, 61 ; Buschius of Hildesheim records pewter in Saxon convents, 68 ; pewter in the convents at Erfurth, *ib*. ; Martin Harscher, a noted German craftsman, 1523, 75 ; Melchior Koch, a Nuremberg craftsman, makes an alloy resembling gold, 1564, 82 ; pewterers claim to make every article produced by gold- or silversmiths, 1573, 84 ; Peter Schmitt's candlesticks ob-

German Pewter—*cont.*
jected to by goldsmiths of Nuremberg, 84 ; development of decorated ware in the sixteenth century, 92 ; salver of Nuremberg a reproduction of Briot's Temperantia salver, 95
Ghent, references, 58, 59, 126
Gilbert, W. S., references, 2, 101
Gill Measure. See Measures
Gloucester Candlestick. See Candlesticks
Goldsmiths' Company purchase pewter, 1470, 67 ; their marks imitated in 1635, 99
Goupil, Jehan, of Tours, sells pewter to Charles VII. of France, 64
Gowland, Mr., on the treatment of pewter by the Japanese, 143 ; references, 9, 10, 11, 14, 15, 48, 50
Gray, Master, of Dundee Corporation, 85
Grey, Ninian, works at two trades, 113
Guild Cups. See Tankards
Guildhall, London, reference, 13
Guildhall Museum, London, Anglo-Saxon specimens at, 52
Guillebert of Metz, a noted French craftsman, 64

Half-Gill Measure. See Measures
Half-Glass Measure. See Measures
Half Mutchkin. See Measures
Halliday, J. E., his "Terrier," or inventory of the Diocese of Llandaff, reference, 128
Halomesnil, Jean de, bénitier possessed by, 60
Hammermen : called "Sadware" men, 27 ; articles made by, 28 ; their work fashioned by hammering, 33 ; incorporated at Perth, 75 ; at Cannongate, *ib*. ; patron saint St. Eloi, *ib*. ; incorporated at Glasgow, 76 ; earliest ordi-

Hammermen—*cont.*
nances at St. Andrew's, 77; James V. ratifies "Seal of Cause" of the Cannongate, 1540, *ib.*; apprentices of Perth forbidden to play on the Inch, 79; first "Seal of Cause" granted to Aberdeen, 1579, 84; Stirling records imperfect, 89; pewterers not mentioned in Glasgow records before 1648, 100; last Cannongate enrolment, 111; craft combines with other trades at Perth, 1747, 115; meetings still held at Aberdeen, Dundee, Perth, and Stirling, 119
Hancock, Samuel, London Company's attitude towards, 1690, 107
Harrison's "Description of England," quoted, 12, 29, 39, 86
Harscher, Martin, a famous German craftsman, reference, 75
Hemeron Pierre a French craftsman 1507, 73
Henry VII., references, 72, 90
Herb-Cannisters :
Dutch ; seventeenth century ; mark, a standing figure ; *plate* LXXXVI, ii ; 118, 161
Dutch ; marked 1766, a Cupid in profile blowing a horn ; PSB ; *plate* LXXXVI, iv ; 118, 161
Herodotus, reference, 31
Hiring out articles a profitable branch of the trade, 39
Hollow-ware, finishing process, 36
Hollow-ware men, references, 27, 69
Hope, Mr. St. John, reference, 96
Horne, John, of Snow Hill, his mark on early English Measure ; *plate* IX, i ; 12, 158
Hoskyns, Thomas, of Oxted, his pewter in 1615, 97
Hungary, Clement of, list of his pewter vessels, alluded to, 57

ICELAND, Pocket Communion Service bought in ; *plate* XXX, i ; 45
Ictis, named by old historians, supposed to be either St. Michael's Mount, Falmouth, Weymouth, or the Isle of Wight, 32
Ink-Stands, &c. :
Ink-pot, Scotch ; no mark ; *plate* XCVIII, i ; 133, 162
Inkstand ; *plate* XL, iii ; 60, 162
—— *plate* LXXXIII, v ; 117
—— late eighteenth century ; *plate* XCIX, ii ; 134, 162
—— French ; eighteenth century ; *plate* XCV, ii ; 132, 162
—— Italian ; *plate* XCVIII, ii ; 133, 162
Isabella of Bavaria, her purchase for the Hotel St. Pol in 1401, 63
Isle of Wight, reference, 32

JAMES V. persuades foreign craftsmen to settle in Scotland, 1539, 77
James VI. grants charter to the crafts, 1581, 85 ; references, 97, 83
Japan, spoons seen by Mr. Gowland at Nara, 50
Japanese treatment of pewter, 15, 143
Jeandun, Jean de, his reference to French decorators, 56
John II. of France, his pewter, 1351, 58
John, King, reference, 54
Johnson, Dr., reference, 7
Jonson, Ben, reference, 139
Jugs. See Flagons
Jupe, John, his defiant attitude towards the London Company, 1736, 113

KOCH, Melchior, his alloy resembling gold, 82

INDEX

Kriswick, chalice and paten from, *plate* XXI, iii, 30
Kwammu, Emperor of Japan, reference, 50

LADLES :
   Laton slip-top Ladle, handle of hexagonal section seventeenth century ; *plate* XX, iv ; 29, 151
   —— slip-top Ladle, found in the City of London ; has remains of tin plating ; seventeenth century ; *plate* XX, v ; 29
   —— slip-top Ladle, found in Suffolk ; seventeenth century ; *plate* XX, vi ; 29
   —— slip-top Ladle, found in London ; seventeenth century ; *plate* XX, vii ; 29, 150
   Soup Ladle, marked John Yates ; *plate* XI, iii ; 14, 152
   —— marked Askberry, &c. ; *plate* XI, iv ; 14, 152
   Toddy Ladles, marked John Yates, &c. ; *plate* XI, i ; 14, 152
"La Grande Mademoiselle" (the Duchesse de Montpensier), 103

Lamps :
   Rarely found in good condition, 154
   Lamp Time-Keepers ; seventeenth century; *plate* XXXVIII, i-v ; 58, 155
   Oil Lamp ; German ; eighteenth century ; *plate* XXXVII, i ; 56, 154
   —— Lamps ; German ; eighteenth century; *plate* XXXVII, iv, v ; 56, 154
   Spirit-Lamp ; *plate* LXXXV, vi ; 118, 161
La Rue, French craftsman, 60 ;

"Laver," the, its first appearance, 97. See Church Vessels &c.
Le Bœuf, Jean, in 1396 forestalls an incident recorded in "Pickwick," 61
Le Peautrer, Nicholas, establishment of the craft in London proved by his will, 1347, 58
Lea, Francis, fined, 1668, for making inferior toys, 105
Limoges, composition of pewter at, 13
"Livres des Mestiers" of Charles V. pewter bottles mentioned in, 69
London, spoons found in, *plate* XII, ii, iv-viii, 16 ; *plate* XIII, ii, v, vii, viii, 18 ; *plate* XIV, i, iii, vii, viii, 20 ; *plate* XV, ii, iv, vi, 21 ; *plate* XVI, ii, vii, viii, ix, 22 ; *plate* XVII, i, iv-viii, 24 ; *plate* XVIII, i, iii, 26 ; *plate* XIX, vii, 28 ; *plate* XX, i, vii, 29
Louise of Savoy, reference, 74
Louis XIV. sends his plate to the Mint, 102, 108
Loving Cup. See Tankards

MACHINES, their use discouraged by early craftsmen, 36
Marks and Marking : vessels to be stamped with quality mark and private "touch," 37 ; Mons marks in 1467, 67 ; marking made compulsory by Act of Parliament, 1503, 72 ; enacted in Scotland, 1567, 83 ; hall-marking of tavern measures ordained by Dundee guild, 1614, 96 ; compulsory in Scotland, 1641, 100 ; plates of "touches" at Pewterers' Hall, 121 ; few marks on existing specimens, 121 ; confusion caused by the authorities, 122 ; Edinburgh "touches," 124 ; advice to owners of specimens with

175

Marks and Marking—*cont.*
private "touches," 125; marks in general misleading and confusing, 125, 127; Nuremberg marks the most reliable, 127; reasons for the absence of marks, 128; marks, where legible, of spoons on *plates* XII–XX. See special *plates* CIV, CV, CVI, 148, 150, 152
Marlowe, Christopher, reference, 138
Martin, abbot, 1186–1191, early pewter plaque recording name and title, 53
Massé, Mr., "Catalogue of the Pewter Exhibition" organised by him at Clifford's Inn Hall, references, 127, 147; alluded to, 9, 16, 65, 96, 121, 125
Maxwell, Stephen, of Glasgow uses London stamp, 124
Measures:
Comparison of Scotch and English, 132
Measure; *plate* LXXXIII; 117
Measures; *plate* LVI, i-v; 78, 158
Measure, temp. Charles II. found in Parliament Street; *plate* XXX, iii; 45
—— English; seventeenth century; *plate* LXXIV, iv.; 106
—— English; early eighteenth century; *plate* LXXII, iii; 94
—— English; early eighteenth century; mark, "John Horne," &c.; *plate* IX, i; 12, 158
—— English; early eighteenth century; *plate* XLIV, ii; 64, 158
—— English; early eighteenth century; *plate* XLIV, iii; 64, 158
—— English; eighteenth century; *plate* L, iii; 74, 157

Measures—*cont.*
Measures English; eighteenth century; *plate* LVIII, vi; 82, 158
—— eighteenth century; *plate* LXXIX, v; 114
Measures, French, A set of, *plate* XLIX, 86
—— Scotch; eighteenth century; *plate* LV, i-iv; 78, 158
Measure, German; *plate* V, i; 10
—— or Tankard, German late seventeenth century *plate* LIV; 78
Gill Measure; no marks; *plate* XXXI, vi; 46, 158
—— Measure, Modern, mark VR Crowned; *plate* XXXI, ii; 46, 158
Half Gill Measure; marked like Mutchkin but with two oval stamps instead of Glas. and shield; *plate* XXXI, v; 46, 158
Quarter Gill Measure; Glasgow mark; *plate* LXXXII, ix; 116
Half Mutchkin Measure; marked Imperial crown Standard, &c.; *plate* XXXI, iii; 46, 158
Old Half Glass Measure; no marks; *plate* XXXI, iv; 46, 158
Tappit Hen.; eighteenth century; *plate* LX; 85, 158
—— —— Scotch; eighteenth century; *plate* VIII, ii; 13, 132, 158
—— Hens; *plate* LIX, i, ii, iii; 84, 158
Wine Measures, German; eighteenth century; *plate* LVII, ii, iii; 80, 158
Michelet the Breton, a French craftsman of 1380, 59, 60
Midhurst, Communion Flagon from, frontispiece; *plate* XXI, ii; 30, 153

INDEX

Milk Jugs :
    English ; late eighteenth century ; *plate* LXXVI, iii ; 109
    —— early nineteenth century; *plate* XCII, i ; 126
Miscellaneous objects, 162
Moncel, Isabel de, a French craftswoman, 1395, 61
Mons, a Belgian centre of the craft, 58, 67
Mont St. Michel, early pewter plaques found in coffins at, 53
Monteith, James, a craftsman, 1649, his claim for making bullets, 101
Montpelier, composition of pewter there in 1437, 13 ; reference, 65
Montrousti, Jehan de, supplies pewter to Isabella of Bavaria, 63
Moulds : list made by Mr. Welch, 33 ; new names appearing in a further York list, 35
Moyes, Mr. James one of the last Edinburgh pewterers, 118
Mugs :
    Mug, early nineteenth century ; *plate* CIII, iv ; 142
    —— William IV. ; *plate* CIII, i ; 142
    —— with handle, English ; early eighteenth century; *plate* LXXIV, iii;106
Mustard Pots :
    Mustard Pot ; *plate* v, iv ; 10, 111
    —— English ; seventeenth century ; *plate* LXV, i ; 94
    —— English ; early eighteenth century ; *plate* XCVII, iii ; 133
    —— eighteenth century; *plate* LXXIX, i ; 114
    —— late eighteenth century ; *plate* LXXIX, iii ; 114

Mustard Pots—*cont.*
    Mustard Pot ; marked with a figure floating in the air; *plate* XC, iii ; 125
    Mustard Pots ; *plate* VI, v, vi, vii ; 10, 111
    —— seventeenth and eighteenth centuries ; *plate* LXXX, i-vi ; 114, 161

NEWGATE Street, Rat-tailed spoon found at ; *plate* XIX, ii ; 28
Nightingale, Rev. J. E., "Church Plate of Norfolk," reference, 100
Northampton, Lord, his pewter in 1614, 97
Northumberland, an Earl of, in the habit of hiring pewter vessels, 40
Norwich, Seal-headed spoon found at, *plate* XX, viii, 29
Nuremberg, composition of pewter at, 1576, 13 ; marks the most reliable, 127 ; references, 57, 126, 127

OLD Half Glass Measure. See Measures
Oriental Dagger. See Dagger

PARLIAMENT Street, Whitehall, Measure found in ; *plate* XXX, iii ; 45
Paten. See Church Vessels, &c.
Peg Tankard. See Tankards
Penny, Edmund, gives a Church vessel, 1609, 95
Pepper-Boxes and Pots :
    Pepper-box ; *plate* v, ii ; 10
    —— eighteenth century ; *plate* LXXIX, iv ; 114
    Pepper-boxes ; *plate* VI, i, iii, iv ; 10, 111
    Pepper-Pot, English ; eighteenth century ; *plate* XCVII, i ; 133

Pepper-Boxes and Pots—*cont.*
   Pepper-Pot ; English ; early nineteenth century ; *plate* XCVII, ii ; 133
   —— seventeenth and eighteenth century ; *plate* LXXXI, i-vi ; 114, 161
Pepys, Samuel, buys a pewter cistern, 1667, 105
Pewter : its disuse for domestic and other purposes, 3 ; derivation of the term, 7 ; composition of English " fine pewter," 11 ; its composition according to Harrison the historian, 12 ; rough and ready tests for ascertaining its quality, 16 ; tests used by French pewterers, 17 ; how it was wrought, 24 ; all the metals employed home products, 32
Pewterers' Company oppose " Crooked-lane men," 105
Pewterers' Hall, 1640 the earliest date on "touch" plate preserved there, 100 ; the last " touch " registered there in 1824, 118
" Pied de Biche " specimens. See Spoons
Pirley Pig of Dundee : date ; description ; use ; loss, and recovery in 1839, 94
Pitt and Davley, their mark ; *plate* IX, iii ; 12
Plates :
   Plate, one of six ; English ; eighteenth century ; *plate* LXV, iii ; 103, 160
   —— one of a set of six, English eighteenth century ; stamped with initials ICB and IBB ; *plate* LVIII, iv ; 82, 160
   —— Wavy-Edged, English ; late eighteenth century; one of a set of six; *plate* LXXIII, v ; 104, 160

Plautus, reference to pewter, 45
Pliny, his reference to tin, 31
Plumbum candidum, the ancient term for tin, 31
Plumbum nigrum, the ancient term for lead, 31
Pocket Communion Service. See Church Vessels, &c.
Poitiers, Henry de, Bishop of Troyes, his pewter, 59
Porringers :
   Porringer, French ; probably seventeenth century ; *plate* XXVIII, iii ; 42, 160
   Porringers ; *plate* LXX, i, ii, iii ; 100, 160
Poullett, Sir Richard, his "sallet pewter dishes " of 1618, 34
Protective safe-guards of the old craftsmen, 38
Purling, Major, his invention called Silvorum, 103
" Puritan " handle. See Spoons
Pyx. See Church Vessels, &c.

QUAIGH, 132, 136
Quarter-gill Measure. See Measures

" RAT-TAIL " pattern. See Spoons
Read, C. K., references, 46, 48
Regulations of the early craftsmen designed to protect the purchaser and to insure good workmanship, 24, 25 ; the old regulations summarised, 26 ; days and hours of manufacture, 37 ; lids of stoneware vessels, 80 ; apprentices, 1564, 82 ; sale of goods, 39
" Revue des Arts Decoratifs," early post-Roman Chalice, now destroyed, reproduced in, 52
Rheims, Archbishop of, his bequest, 1389, 61
Rhynd, Janet, her generous gift to the Edinburgh Trade Incorporation, 78

INDEX

Rice-Boiler ; French ; eighteenth century ; *plate* LVIII, iii ; 82, 162

Richard Cœur de Lion, Church plate melted to procure his ransom, 53

Richard III., King, reference, 90

Roman pewter, divergent results of analysis, 9 ; the discoveries at Appleshaw, Icklingham, Sutton, and Colchester, 45 ; conjectures as to date, 49 ; effects of the Roman withdrawal on the industry, 51

Rouen, references, 58, 60, 63

Ruprecht, Sebaldus, German craftsman, 1389, 61

SACRAMENTAL Cruets. See Church Vessels, &c.

Sadware, how fashioned, 36

Sadware men. See Hammermen

St. Cyr, pewter at the convent of, 68

St. Eloi, the patron saint of Scotch Hammermen, 75, 84

St. Martin, pewter at the Cistercian convent of, 68

St. Michael's Mount, reference, 32

St. Stephen's, Coleman Street, London, pewter vessels in use, 1467, at, 67

Salt-Cellars and Boxes :
Salt-Box ; *plate* CI, ii ; 138
Salt-Cellars ; *plate* LXXXIII, ii ; 117, 161
—— *plate* LXXXIV, i-v ; 117, 161
—— marked with crowned X ; *plate* VI, viii-xii ; 10, 111
Salt-Cellar, English ; eighteenth century ; *plate* L, ii ; 74
—— eighteenth century; *plate* LXXIX, ii ; 114
—— Cromwellian ; *plate* LXXXII, iii ; 116, 161

Salt-Cellars—*cont.*
Salt-Cellar, English ; *plate* LXXXII, v ; 116, 161
—— English ; Georgian ; *plate* LXXXII, vii ; 116, 161

Salver, Wavy-Edged, with feet, Dutch ; late eighteenth century ; *plate* LXXIII, i, 104, 160 ; salver of Nuremberg, 1611, a reproduction of Briot's Temperantia salver, 95

Sampson, Patrick, references, 110, 111

Sandarach, or *Callitris quadrivalsis*, used for coating moulds, 35

Schmitt, Peter, a German craftsman, 84

Schoper, Harman, "Treatise on Industries," quoted, 84

Scotch Pewter : Scotland's advance in the craft retarded by the absence of native tin, 69 ; manufacture first recorded in Edinburgh 1496, 70 ; arrangements of Guilds differ from those in England, *ib.* ; first recorded incorporation of Hammermen at Perth, 1518, 75 ; at Cannongate, 1535, *ib.*; St. Eloi the patron saint, 75 ; first recorded incorporation of Glasgow Hammermen, 76 ; earliest ordinances of St. Andrews Hammermen, 77 ; James V. persuades foreign craftsmen to settle in Scotland, and ratifies the "Seal of Cause" of the Cannongate Hammermen, *ib.* ; measures reimposed, 1543, to secure competent craftsmen, 78 ; the Edinburgh Corporation become owners of the Chapel of St. Mary Magdalen, 78 ; Perth apprentices forbidden to play on the Inch, 79 ; Church plate of St. Giles', Edinburgh, removed for

179

OLD PEWTER

Scotch Pewter—*cont.*
safety, 81 ; Perth apprentices wishing to become masters present a football to the Guild, 81 ; disappearance of much pre-Reformation Church plate, 82 ; marks enacted, 1567, 83 ; Dundee stoups ordered to be officially marked, *ib.*; first " Seal of Cause " granted to Aberdeen Hammermen, 84 ; James VI. grants charter, 1581, raising crafts to the level of merchants, 85 ; first record of the Dundee Incorporation, *ib.*; records of the Stirling Hammermen, 1596–1620, more than usually imperfect, 89 ; continued growth of the craft in Scotland during the sixteenth century, 92 ; date, description, and use of the Pirley Pig, 94 ; its loss and recovery, *ib.*; Hall-marking ordained, 1614, by Dundee Guild, 96 ; effects of the Revolution of 1617 in the Church of Scotland, 97 ; first appearance of the "laver," *ib.*; no pewterer in St. Andrews Guild until 1619, 98 ; effects of the Church troubles in 1638 on the craft, 99 ; marks made compulsory, 1641, 100 ; pewterers not mentioned in Glasgow records before 1648, 100 ; James Monteith's claim for making bullets, 101 ; penalty in Edinburgh for using bad metal, 103 ; effects of the Restoration on the craft in Scotland, 104 ; Act to prevent the craft from encroaching upon the trade of plumbers, 105 ; interesting Ordinances issued by the Aberdeen Guild, 105 ; quarrel between pewterers and plumbers of Edinburgh, 106 ; effects of

Scotch Pewter—*cont.*
the accession of William III. on Church plate, 106 ; white iron-smiths admitted to the freedom of Aberdeen Guild, 107 ; decline of the craft and threatened absorption by white iron-smiths, 110 ; enrolment of the last pewterer at the Cannongate, 111 ; craftsmen of St. Andrews and Perth fail to preserve their monopoly, 112, 113 ; efforts of Edinburgh white iron-smiths to found a distinct craft, 114 ; Dundee corporation enrols the last pewterer, 115 ; Perth hammermen combine with other trades, *ib.*; effects of the Presbyterians on the craft, 116 ; last pewterers enrolled at Aberdeen and Perth, *ib.*; white iron-smiths openly make pewter articles, *ib.*; St. Andrews pewterers outnumbered by tin-smiths, 117 ; Aberdeen, Dundee, Perth, and Stirling Hammermen still hold meetings but have no executive power, 119
" Seal-headed " pattern. See Spoons
Shakespeare, pewter mentioned by, 87 ; reference, 139
Sharpe, Dr., his Calendar drawn up for the Corporation of the City of London, 58
Shaving-Pot ; English ; *plate* CII, i ; 140
Shoe Buckles, A pair of ; no marks ; *plate* XCVI, ii, iv ; 133, 162
Shokotu, Empress of Japan, reference, 51
Silvorum, Purling's new invention, 103
Skeat, Professor, references, 7, 28
" Slip-top " pattern. See Spoons

INDEX

Smith, Samuel, London, breaks advertising rule, 116
Snuff-Boxes :
 Snuff-Box ; no marks ; *plate* XCVI, v ; 133
 —— no marks ; eighteenth century ; *plate* XCVI, i ; 133, 162
 —— English ; middle eighteenth century ; *plate* XCVII, iv ; 133, 162
 —— Scotch ; no marks ; *plate* XCVI, iii ; 133, 162
Soignies, reference, 60
Soup Ladle. See Ladles
Soup Tureen, Russian ; Archangel mark ; *plate* LXXV ; 108, 161
Spanish Pewter, statutes and regulations drawn up, 1406, at Barcelona, 63
Spice-Box, French ; eighteenth century ; *plate* XXIX, ii ; 44, 162
Spinning, a method of working pewter, 37
Spoons :
 Bronze, found in the City of London; fourteenth century; probably French : *plate* XII, ii ; 16, 148
 —— found in London ; fifteenth century ; *plate* XII, vi ; 16, 148
 —— stem of diamond section, found in London ; fifteenth century ; *plate* XII, vii ; 16, 148
 —— found in London ; fifteenth century (mark, same as No. 2) ; *plate* XII, viii ; 16, 148
 —— rat-tailed ; seventeenth century ; *plate* XIX, viii; 28, 151
Dutch ; *plate* LXXXII, ii, iv, vi, viii, x ; 116
Laton, found in the Thames at Westminster ; four-

Spoons—*cont.*
 teenth century ; *plate* XII, i ; 16, 148
 Laton French ; fourteenth century ; *plate* XII, iii ; 16
 —— found in the Thames in London, stem of diamond section ; early fifteenth century ; *plate* XII, iv ; 16, 148
 —— found in London ; early fifteenth century ; probably French ; *plate* XII, v ; 16, 148
 —— plated with pewter ; found in London ; late seventeenth century ; *plate* XIX, vii ; 28, 151
 —— plated with tin ; seventeenth century ; *plate* XVIII, iv ; 26, 151
 —— with remains of tin plating ; seventeenth century ; *plate* XVIII, v ; 26, 151
 —— plated with tin ; handle "Pied de Biche "(mark same as No. 5) ; *plate* XVIII, vi ; 26, 151
 —— with remains of tin plating ; handle " Pied de Biche " ; seventeenth century ; *plate* XVIII, vii ; 26, 151
 —— rat-tailed ; plated with tin ; handle " Pied de Biche " ; seventeenth century ; *plate* XIX, i ; 28, 151
 —— rat-tailed, found in York Road, Westminster ; plated with tin ; seventeenth century ; *plate* XIX, iii ; 28, 151
 —— rat-tailed, found in York Road, Westminster ; handle" Pied de Biche" ; seventeenth century ; *plate* XVIII, viii ; 26, 151

OLD PEWTER

Spoons—*cont.*
  Laton, seal-top, found in London ; seventeenth century ; *plate* XVII, i ; 24, 150
  —— seal-top ; seventeenth century ; *plate* XVII, ii ; 24, 150
  —— seal-top ; seventeenth century ; *plate* XVII, iii ; 24, 150
  —— seal-top, found in London ; seventeenth century ; *plate* XVII, iv ; 24, 150
  —— seal-top, found in London ; seventeenth century ; *plate* XVII, v ; 24, 150
  —— seal-top, found in London ; seventeenth century ; *plate* XVII, vi ; 24, 150
  —— seal-top, found in London ; seventeenth century ; *plate* XVII, vii ; 24, 150
  —— seal-top, found in London ; seventeenth century ; *plate* XVII, viii ; 24, 150
  —— seal-top, with remains of tin-plating, found at Norwich ; seventeenth century ; *plate* XX, viii ; 29, 150
  —— slip-top, plated with tin ; found in London ; seventeenth century ; *plate* XVIII, i ; 26, 151
  —— slip-top, found at Bermondsey ; has remains of tin plating ; seventeenth century ; *plate* XVI, v ; 22
  —— slip-top, found at Bermondsey ; seventeenth century ; *plate* XVI, vi ; 22, 149

Spoons—*cont.*
  Laton, slip-top, found in London ; has remains of tin plating ; seventeenth century ; *plate* XVI, vii ; 22
  —— slip-top, found in London ; seventeenth century ; *plate* XVIII, iii ; 26, 151
  —— spoon, found in London ; stem of hexagonal section ; seventeenth century ; *plate* XIV, iii ; 20, 150
  —— spoon, with Apostle top ; seventeenth century ; *plate* XIV, iv ; 20, 150
  —— dog-nose gravy spoon, plated with tin ; seventeenth century ; *plate* XX, ii ; 29, 150
  Pewter, found in London ; sixteenth century ; *plate* XIV, i ; 20, 150
  —— seventeenth century ; *plate* XIV, ii ; 20, 151
  —— found in London ; seventeenth century ; *plate* XIV, vii ; 20
  —— found in London ; late eighteenth century ; *plate* XX, i ; 29, 152
  —— found in Bermondsey, late eighteenth century ; *plate* XX, iii ; 29, 152
  —— with Apostle top, found in London ; sixteenth century ; *plate* XIV, viii ; 20, 150
  —— rat-tailed, found in Newgate Street ; handle " Pied de Biche " ; seventeenth century ; *plate* XIX, ii ; 28, 151
  —— rat-tailed, found in Bermondsey ; seventeenth century ; *plate* XIX, iv ; 28, 151

INDEX

Spoons—*cont.*
Pewter, rat, tailed, found in Bermondsey ; seventeenth century ; *plate* XIX, v ; 28, 151
—— rat-tailed, seventeenth century ; *plate* XIX, vi ; 28, 151
—— rat-tailed chocolate spoon, found in the Wandle, at Wandsworth ; seventeenth century ; *plate* XIX, ix ; 28, 151
—— seal-headed, hexagonal, found at Bermondsey ; sixteenth century ; *plate* XIV, v ; 20, 150
—— slip-top found at Bermondsey, stem of hexagonal section ; fifteenth century ; *plate* XIII, i ; 18, 149
—— slip-top, found in London ; sixteenth century ; *plate* XIII, ii ; 18, 149
—— slip-top, sixteenth century ; *plate* XIII, iii ; 18, 149
—— slip-top ; seventeenth century ; *plate* XIII, iv ; 18
—— slip-top, found in London ; sixteenth century ; *plate* XIII, v ; 18, 149
—— slip-top, found in York Road, Westminster ; sixteenth century; *plate* XIII, vi ; 18, 149
—— slip-top, found in London ; sixteenth century ; *plate* XIII, vii ; 18, 149
—— slip-top, found in London ; seventeenth century ; *plate* XIII, viii ; 18

Spoons—*cont.*
Pewter, slip-top, found in York Road, Westminster; sixteenth century ; *plate* XV, i (same mark as No. 6); *plate* XIII ; 21, 149
—— slip-top, found in London ; sixteenth century (same mark as No. 6, *plate* XIII); *plate* XV, ii ; 21, 149
—— slip-top, the same as No. 2 ; *plate* XV, iii ; 21, 149
—— slip-top, found in London ; sixteenth century ; *plate* XV, iv ; 21, 149
—— slip-top, sixteenth century ; *plate* XV, v ; 21, 149
—— slip-top, found in London ; sixteenth century (same mark as No. 2); *plate* XV, vi ; 21, 149
—— slip-top ; sixteenth century ; *plate* XV, vii ; 21, 149
—— found in Bermondsey ; sixteenth century; *plate* XV, viii ; 21, 149
—— slip-top, found in London ; sixteenth century ; *plate* XVI, ix ; 22, 149
—— slip-top, found in London ; sixteenth century ; *plate* XVI, viii ; 22
—— slip-top, found at Bermondsey ; sixteenth century ; *plate* XVI, i ; 22, 149
—— slip-top, found in London ; sixteenth century ; *plate* XVI, ii ; 22, 149
—— slip-top, found at Ber-

Spoons—*cont.*
  mondsey; sixteenth century; *plate* XVI, iii; 22, 149
  Pewter, slip-top, found at Bermondsey; sixteenth century; *plate* XVI, iv; 22, 149
  —— slip-top, found at Bermondsey; seventeenth century; *plate* XVIII, ii; 26, 151
  Sacramental Spoon. See Church Vessels, &c.
  Table-Spoons, three, marked John Yates, &c.; *plate* XI, v; 14, 152
  Tea Spoon, marked AI &c.; *plate* XI, vi; 14, 152
Stannaries, Edward I. confirms Charter to, 56
Steele, Richard, reference, 139
Students' Beer Jug. See Beer Jugs
Suetonius, his reference to the substitution of pewter for silver vessels, 45
Sugar-Basins, Castors, &c.:
  Sugar-Basin; English; early nineteenth century; *plate* XCII, ii; 126
  —— Belgian; *plate* CII, v; 140
  Sugar-Box and Cover, Dutch; dated 1751; *plate* XC, ii; 125, 162
  Sugar-Castor; *plate* LXXXIII, iii; 117
  —— marked with Cupid, &c.; *plate* VIII, ii; 10
  Sugar-Sifters; eighteenth century; *plate* LXXXV, i, ii; 118
  Sugar Sprinkler, Belgian; *plate* CII, ii; 140
  —— Sprinkler, Belgian; *plate* CII, iv; 140

TABLE Plate, 161
Table Spoons. See Spoons
Tankards and Cups:
  Cup, on lid 1721, &c.; *plate* XLII, i; 62, 156
  —— inscribed Johannes George Reichel, &c., 1693; *plate* XLII, iii; 62, 156
  —— German Guild, seventeenth century; *plate* XXXII, ii; 48, 156
  —— Scotch; eighteenth century; *plate* XLI, i; 61, 156
  Loving Cup; English; *plate* XXVIII, i; 42, 153, 156
  —— eighteenth century; *plate* XLI, ii; 61, 156
  Peg Tankard, Danish; with engraved decoration inscribed Kleinreide, &c.; *plate* XLVIII, i; 70
  Tankard; late eighteenth century; *plate* CIII, iii; 142, 157
  —— engraved with IAM beneath an anchor, &c.; English; eighteenth century; *plate* IX, iii; 12, 157
  —— English; early eighteenth century; *plate* LXXIV, i; 106
  —— English; eighteenth century; *plate* LXXIV, v; 106
  —— English; eighteenth century; *plate* XCIII, ii; 128, 157
  —— Flemish; seventeenth century; *plate* X, i; 13
  —— French; eighteenth century; *plate* X, iii; 13
  —— German Guild; dated 1645; *plate* XLIX, iii; 72, 157

INDEX

Tankards and Cups—*cont.*
  Tankard; German; eighteenth century; *plate* XLV, ii; 68, 157
  —— Scotch; eighteenth century; marked "Galbraith Glasgow"; *plate* XLIV, i; 64, 157
  Cup, Swedish, 1844; marks, Arms of Sweden, &c.; *plate* XLVIII, iii; 70, 157
  Tankards, German Guild; *plate* LII, i, ii, iii; 76
  —— German Guild; seventeenth to eighteenth century; *plate* LIII, i, ii, iii; 77, 159
  —— German; seventeenth century; *plate* XLVI, i-iv; 68
  —— German; seventeenth and eighteenth centuries; *plate* XLVII, i, ii, iii; 68
  —— German, A Pair of eighteenth century; *plate* LI; 74, 159
  Wine Cups; eighteenth century; no marks; *plate* XLI, iii, iv; 61, 156
Taper-Holder. See Candlesticks
Tappit-Hen. See Measures
Tea-Pots:
  Tea-Pot; eighteenth century; *plate* XCIV, ii; 130
  —— early nineteenth century; *plate* LXXXVIII, i; 122, 161
  —— early nineteenth century; *plate* XCIV, i; 130
  —— Dutch; eighteenth century; *plate* LXXXIX, i; 124
  —— English; *plate* XCIII, i; 128
  —— English; early nineteenth century; *plate* XCII, iii; 126

Tea-Pots—*cont.*
  Tea-Pot, Flemish; eighteenth century; *plate* LXXXIX, iii; 124
Temperance salver by Briot, references, 79, 95
Tests for ascertaining the quality of pewter, 17, 16
Tin: reputation of English pewter due to its superior quality, 30; early Biblical and Classical references to, 30, 31; craft in Scotland retarded by its absence, 69; mentioned by Shakespeare, 87; London Company privileged to charge royalty on, 1598, 90
Tobacco-Boxes:
  Tobacco-Box; no marks; *plate* XCVIII, iii; 133
  —— eighteenth century; *plate* XCIV, iii; 130, 162
  —— English; eighteenth century; *plate* LXXIV, vi; 106, 162
  —— French; eighteenth century; *plate* XCV, iii; 132, 162
Toddy-Ladles. See Ladles
Torigny, Robert de (1154–1186), early pewter plaque recording his name and title, 53
Tottenham Court Road, Wine Taster dug up in, *plate* LVII, 80
Trays:
  Tray; eighteenth century; *plate* XL, ii; 60
  —— or Salver, Dutch; *plate* LXXVI, ii; 109, 162
Triflers, workers in the metal known as "trifle," 27, 28; in 1612 included hollow-ware in their output, 96
Troyes, references, 59, 60

URNS:
  Urn, Dutch; *plate* LXXXVII, i; 121, 161

Urns—*cont.*
  Urn, Dutch ; *plate* LXXXVII, iii ; 121, 161
  —— French ; *plate* LXXXVII, ii ; 121, 161
Uvedale, Lady Elizabeth, her bequest of pewter, 1487, 69

VEGETABLE DISH ; English ; late eighteenth century ; *plate* LXXVI, i ; 109, 161
Vessels and Dish, Roman, found by Rev. C. H. Engleheart ; *plate* III, i, ii, iii ; 4, 47, 48, 49
Victoria and Albert Museum, Gloucester Candlestick at, *plate* IV, 5, 54 ; specimens of decorated pewter at, 80 ; Nuremberg Salver there, a reproduction of Briot's Temperantia Salver, 95. See also *frontispiece* and *plates* IX XXI, XXII, XLVIII, XLIX, LIV, LVII, XC
Vinegar Cruet ; *plate* LXXXIII, iv ; 117, 161

WALTHAM Abbey Church; pewter purchased for, 80
Wandsworth, rat-tailed pewter chocolate spoon found at, *plate* XIX, ix ; 28
Water-Jugs :
  Hot-Water Jug ; Dutch ; early eighteenth century ; *plate* LXXII, ii ; 94
  Water-Jug ; English ; eighteenth century ; *plate* LVIII, ii ; 82, 159
  —— English ; eighteenth century ; *plate* LXXVI, iv ; 109
  —— English ; late eighteenth century ; *plate* LXXIII, iv ; 104

Welch, Mr., "History of the Pewterers' Company," 26 ; list of moulds, 33 ; reference, 95
Westminster, spoons found at ; *plates* XII, i, 16 ; XIII, vi, 18 ; XV, i, 21 ; XVIII, viii, 26 ; XIX, iii ; 28
Weymouth, reference, 32
White iron-smiths, their absorption of the craft, 107, 110, 112, 113, 116, 117
William III. compelled to strike part of his coinage in pewter, 108 ; reference, 106
Wine Measure. See Measures
Wine Taster, English ; seventeenth century ; dug up in Tottenham Court Road ; *plate* LVII, i ; 80, 160
Wolsey, Cardinal, plate belonging to, 91
Woman, A, belongs to the craft in the thirteenth century, 55
Wood, Mr. Ingleby, "Scottish Pewter-Ware and Pewterers," reference, 26 ; "Church Vessels before and after the Reformation," reference, 133 ; references, 69, 76, 81, 89, 98, 124, 125, 131, 158
Wright, James, of St. Andrews reference, 117

YATES, JOHN, his mark on Spoons and Ladles, *plate* XI, iii, v ; 14, 152
York, the principal trading place for the North of England in 1419, 64, 77
Yorkshire, Patens from a Church in, *plate* XXII, iii ; 32

www.ingramcontent.com/pod-product-compliance
Lightning Source LLC
Chambersburg PA
CBHW070722160426
43192CB00009B/1278